P9-DMS-046

THE RIGHT TO BE LAZY

AND OTHER STUDIES

BY
PAUL LAFARGUE

Translated by CHARLES H. KERR

Fredonia Books
Amsterdam, The Netherlands

The Right to be Lazy and Other Studies

by
Paul Lafargue

ISBN: 1-58963-945-6

Reprinted from the 1907 edition

Fredonia Books
Amsterdam, The Netherlands
http://www.fredoniabooks.com

In order to make original editions of historical works available to scholars at an economical price, this facsimile of the original edition of 1907 is reproduced from the best available copy and has been digitally enhanced to improve legibility, but the text remains unaltered to retain historical authenticity.

PREFACE

M. Thiers, at a private session of the commission on primary education of 1849, said: "I wish to make the influence of the clergy all-powerful because I count upon it to propagate that good philosophy which teaches man that he is here below to suffer, and not that other philosophy which on the contrary bids man to enjoy." M. Thiers was stating the ethics of the capitalist class, whose fierce egoism and narrow intelligence he incarnated.

The Bourgeoisie, when it was struggling against the nobility sustained by the clergy, hoisted the flag of free thought and atheism; but once triumphant, it changed its tone and manner and today it uses religion to support its economic and political supremacy. In the fifteenth and sixteenth centuries, it had joyfully taken up the pagan tradition and glorified the flesh and its passions, reproved by Christianity; in our days, gorged with goods and with pleasures, it denies the teachings of its thinkers like Rabelais and Diderot, and preaches abstinence to the wage-workers. Capitalist ethics, a pitiful parody on Christian ethics, strikes with its anathema the flesh of the laborer; its ideal is to reduce the producer to the smallest number of needs, to suppress his joys and his passions and to condemn him to play the part of a machine turning out work without respite and without thanks.

The revolutionary socialists must take up again the battle fought by the philosophers and pamphleteers of the bourgeoisie; they must march up to the assault of the ethics and the social theories of capitalism; they must demolish in the heads of the class which they call to action the prejudices sown in them by the ruling class; they must proclaim in the faces of the hypocrites of all ethical systems that the earth shall cease to be the vale of tears for the laborer; that in the communist society of the future, which we shall establish "peaceably if we may, forcibly if we must," the impulses of men will be given a free rein, for "all these impulses are by nature good, we have nothing to avoid but their misuse and their excesses,*" and they will not be avoided except by their mutual counter-

* Descartes. "Les Passions de l'ame."

balancing, by the harmonious development of the human organism, for as Dr. Beddoe says, "It is only when a race reaches its maximum of physical development, that it arrives at its highest point of energy and moral vigor." Such was also the opinion of the great naturalist Charles Darwin.*

This refutation of the "Right to Work" which I am republishing with some additional notes appeared in the weekly "Egalité", 1880, second series.

P. L.

Sainte-Pélagie Prison, 1883.

---

* Doctor Beddoe. "Memoirs of the Anthropological Society.
Charles Darwin. "Descent of Man."

TABLE OF CONTENTS

THE RIGHT TO BE LAZY

Let us be lazy in everything, except in loving and drinking, except in being lazy.
—Lessing.

I.

A DISASTROUS DOGMA.

A strange delusion possesses the working classes of the nations where capitalist civilization holds its sway. This delusion drags in its train the individual and social woes which for two centuries have tortured sad humanity. This delusion is the love of work, the furious passion for work, pushed even to the exhaustion of the vital force of the individual and his progeny. Instead of opposing this mental aberration, the priests, the economists and the moralists have cast a sacred halo over work. Blind and finite men, they have wished to be wiser than their God; weak and contemptible men, they have presumed to rehabilitate what their God had cursed. I, who do not profess to be a Christian, an economist or a moralist, I appeal from their judgement to that of their God; from the preachings of their religious, economics or freethought ethics, to the frightful consequences of work in capitalist society.

In capitalist society work is the cause of all intellectual degeneracy, of all organic deformity. Compare the thorough-bred in Rothschild's stables, served by a retinue of bipeds, with the heavy brute of the Norman farms which plows the earth, carts the manure, hauls the crops. Look at the noble savage whom the missionaries of trade and the traders of religion have not yet corrupted with Christianity, syphilis and the dogma of work, and then look at our miserable slaves of machines.*

* European explorers pause in wonder before the physical beauty and the proud bearing of the men of primitive races, not soiled by what Paeppig calls "the poisonous breath of civilization." Speaking of the aborigines of the Oceanic Islands, Lord George Campbell writes: "There is not a people in the world which strikes one more favorably at first sight. Their smooth skin of a light copper tint, their hair golden and curly, their beautiful and happy faces, in a word, their whole person formed a new and splendid specimen of the 'genus homo'; their physical appearance gave the impression of a race superior to ours." The civilized men of ancient Rome, witness Caesar and Tacitus, regarded with the same admiration the Germans of the communist tribes which invaded the Roman empire. Following Tacitus, Salvien, the priest of the fifth century who received the surname of master of the Bishops, held up the barbarians as an example

When, in our civilized Europe, we would find a trace of the native beauty of man, we must go seek it in the nations where economic prejudices have not yet uprooted the hatred of work. Spain, which, alas, is degenerating, may still boast of possessing fewer factories than we have of prisons and barracks; but the artist rejoices in his admiration of the hardy Andalusian, brown as his native chestnuts, straight and flexible as a steel rod; and the heart leaps at hearing the beg-

---

to civilized Christians: "We are immodest before the barbarians, who are more chaste than we. Even more, the barbarians are wounded at our lack of modesty; the Goths do not permit debauchees of their own nation to remain among them; alone in the midst of them, by the sad privilege of their nationality and their name, the Romans have the right to be impure. (Pederasty was then the height of the fashion among both pagans and Christians.) The oppressed fly to the barbarians to seek for mercy and a shelter." (De Gubernatione Dei.) The old civilization and the rising Christianity corrupted the barbarians of the ancient world, as the old Christianity and the modern capitalist civilization are corrupting the savages of the new world.

M. F. LePlay, whose talent for observation must be recognized, even if we reject his sociological conclusions, tainted with philanthropic and Christian pharisaism, says in his book "Les Ouvriers Européens" (1885): "The Propensity of the Bachkirs for laziness (the Bachkirs are semi-nomadic shepherds of the Asiatic slope of the Ural mountains); the leisure of nomadic life, the habit of meditation which this engenders in the best endowed individuals,—all this often gives them a distinction of manner, a fineness of intelligence and judgement which is rarely to be observed on the same social level in a more developed civilization..... The thing most repugnant to them is agricultural labor: they will do anything rather than accept the trade of a farmer." Agriculture is in fact the first example of servile labor in the history of man. According to biblical tradition, the first criminal, Cain, is a farmer.

gar, superbly draped in his ragged *capa* parleying on terms of equality with the duke of Ossuna. For the Spaniard, in whom the primitive animal has not been atrophied, work is the worst sort of slavery.* The Greeks in their era of greatness had only contempt for work: their slaves alone were permitted to labor: the free man knew only exercises for the body and mind. And so it was in this era that men like Aristotle, Phidias, Aristophanes moved and breathed among the people; it was the time when a handful of heroes at Marathon crushed the hordes of Asia, soon to be subdued by Alexander. The philosophers of antiquity taught contempt for work, that degradation of the free man, the poets sang of idleness, that gift from the Gods:

O Melibae Deus nobis haec otia fecit.†

Jesus, in his sermon on the Mount, preached idleness: "Consider the lilies of the field, how they grow: they toil not, neither do they spin: and yet I say unto you that even Solomon in all his glory was not arrayed like one of these." Jehovah the bearded and angry god, gave his worshipers the supreme example of ideal

---

* The Spanish proverb says: Descanzar es salud. (Rest is healthful.)

† O Melibaeus! a god has granted us this idleness. Virgil's Bucolics. (See appendix.)

laziness; after six days of work, he rests for all eternity.

On the other hand, what are the races for which work is an organic necessity? The Auvergnians; the Scotch, those Auvergnians of the British Isles; the Galicians, those Auvergnians of Spain; the Pomeranians, those Auvergnians of Germany; the Chinese, those Auvergnians of Asia. In our society, which are the classes that love work for work's sake? The peasant proprietors, the little shopkeepers; the former bent double over their fields, the latter crouched in their shops, burrow like the mole in his subterranean passage and never stand up to look at nature leisurely.

And meanwhile the proletariat, the great class embracing all the producers of civilized nations, the class which in freeing itself will free humanity from servile toil and will make of the human animal a free being, — the proletariat, betraying its instincts, despising its historic mission, has let itself be perverted by the dogma of work. Rude and terrible has been its punishment. All its individual and social woes are born of its passion for work.

II.

BLESSINGS OF WORK.

In 1770 at London, an anonymous pamphlet appeared under the title, "An Essay on Trade and Commerce". It made some stir in its time. The author, a great philanthropist, was indignant that "the factory population of England had taken into its head the fixed idea that in their quality of Englishmen all the individuals composing it have by right of birth the privilege of being freer and more independent than the laborers of any country in Europa. This idea may have its usefulness for soldiers, since it stimulates their valor, but the less the factory workers are imbued with it the better for themselves and the state. Laborers ought never to look on themselves as independent of their superiors. It is extremely dangerous to encourage such infatuations in a commercial state like ours, where perhaps seven-eighths of the population have little or no property. The cure will not be complete until our industrial laborers are contented to work six days for the same sum which they now earn in four." Thus, nearly a century before Guizot, work was openly preached in London as a curb to the noble passions of man. "The more my people work, the less vices they will have", wrote Napoleon on May 5th, 1807, from Osterod. "I am the authority....and I should be disposed to order that on Sunday after the hour of service be past, the shops be opened and the laborers return to their work." To root out laziness and curb the sentiments of pride and independence which arise from it, the author of the "Essay on Trade" proposed to imprison the poor in ideal "work-houses", which should become "houses of terror, where they should work fourteen hours a day in such fashion that when meal time was deducted there should remain twelve hours of work full and complete".

Twelve hours of work a day, that is the ideal of the philanthropists and moralists of the eighteenth century. How have we outdone this *nec plus ultra!* Modern factories have become ideal houses of correction in which the toiling masses are imprisoned, in which they are condemned to compulsory work for twelve or fourteen hours, not the men only but also women and children.* And to think that the sons of the heroes of the Terror have allowed themselves to be degraded

---

* At the first Congress of Charities held at Brussels in 1857 one of the richest manufacturers of Marquette, near Lille, M. Scrive, to the plaudits of the members of the congress declared with the noble satisfaction of a duty performed: "We have introduced certain methods of diversion for the children. We teach them to sing during their work, also to count while work-

by the religion of work, to the point of accepting, since 1848, as a revolutionary conquest, the law limiting factory labor to twelve hours. They proclaim as a revolutionary principle the Right to Work. Shame to the French proletariat! Only slaves would have been capable of such baseness. A Greek of the heroic times would have required twenty years of capitalist civilization before he could have conceived such vileness.

And if the miseries of compulsory work and the tortures of hunger have descended upon the proletariat more in number than the locusts of the Bible, it is because the proletariat itself invited them. This work, which in June 1848 the laborers demanded with arms in their hands, this they have imposed on their families; they have delivered up to the barons of industry their wives and children. With their own hands they have demolished their domestic hearths. With their own hands they have dried up the milk of their wives. The unhappy women carrying and nursing their babes have been obliged to go into

---

ing. That distracts them and makes them accept bravely "those twelve hours of labor which are necessary to procure their means of existence." Twelve hours of labor, and such labor, imposed on children less than twelve years old! The materialists will always regret that there is no hell in which to confine these Christian philanthropic murderers of childhood.

the mines and factories to bend their backs and exhaust their nerves. With their own hands they have broken the life and the vigor of their children. Shame on the proletarians! Where are those neighborly housewives told of in our fables and in our old tales, bold and frank of speech, lovers of Bacchus? Where are those buxom girls, always on the move, always cooking, always singing, always spreading life, engendering life's joy, giving painless birth to healthy and vigorous children? .... Today we have factory girls and women, pale drooping flowers, with impoverished blood, with disordered stomachs, with languid limbs .... They have never known the pleasure of a healthful passion, nor would they be capable of telling of it merrily! And the children? Twelve hours of work for children! O, misery. But not all the Jules Simon of the Academy of Moral and Political Science, not all the Germinys of jesuitism, could have invented a vice more degrading to the intelligence of the children, more corrupting of their instincts, more destructive of their organism than work in the vitiated atmosphere of the capitalist factory.

Our epoch has been called the century of work. It is in fact the century of pain, misery and corruption.

And all the while the philosophers, the bourgeois economists—from the painfully confused August Comte to the ludicrously clear Leroy-Beaulieu; the people of bourgeois literature—from the quackishly romantic Victor Hugo to the artlessly grotesque Paul de Kock,—all have intoned nauseating songs in honor of the god Progress, the eldest son of Work. Listen to them and you would think that happiness was soon to reign over the earth, that its coming was already perceived. They rummaged in the dust of past centuries to bring back feudal miseries to serve as a sombre contrast to the delights of the present times. Have they wearied us, these satisfied people, yesterday pensioners at the table of the nobility, today pen-valets of the capitalist class and fatly paid? Have they reckoned us weary of the peasant, such as La Bruyere described him? Well, here is the brilliant picture of proletarian delights in the year of capitalist progress 1840, penned by one of their own men, Dr. Villermé, member of the Institute, the same who in 1848 was a member of that scientific society (Thiers, Cousin, Passy, Blanqui, the academician, were in it), which disseminated among the masses the nonsense of bourgeois economics and ethics.

It is of manufacturing Alsace that Dr. Villermé speaks,—the Alsace of Kestner and Dollfus, those flowers of industrial philanthropy and republicanism. But before the doctor raises up before us his picture of proletarian miseries, let us listen to an Alsatian manufacturer, Mr. Th. Mieg, of the house of Dollfus, Mieg & Co., depicting the condition of the old-time artisan: "At Mulhouse fifty years ago (in 1813, when modern mechanical industry was just arising) the laborers were all children of the soil, inhabiting the town and the surrounding villages, and almost all owning a house and often a little field."* It was the golden age of the laborer. But at that time Alsatian industry did not deluge the world with its cottons, nor make millionaires out of its Dollfus and Koechlin. But twenty-five years after, when Villermé visited Alsace, the modern Minotaur, the capitalist workshop, had conquered the country; in its insatiable appetite for human labor it had dragged the workmen from their hearths, the better to wring them and press out the labor which they contained. It was by thousands that the workers flocked together at the signal of the steam whistle. "A great number", says Villermé, "five thousand

* Speech delivered before the International Society of Practical Studies in Social Economics, at Paris in May 1863, and published in the French "Economist" of the same epoch.

out of seventeen thousand, were obliged by high rents to lodge in neighboring villages. Some of them lived three or four miles from the factory where they worked.*

"At Mulhouse in Dornach, work began at five o'clock in the morning and ended at eight o'clock in the evening, summer and winter. It was a sight to watch them arrive each morning into the city and depart each evening. Among them were a multitude of women, pale, often walking bare-footed through the mud, and who for lack of umbrellas when the rain or snow fell, wore their aprons or skirts turned up over their heads. There was a still larger number of young children, equally dirty, equally pale, covered with rags, greasy from the machine oil which drops on them while they work. They were better protected from the rain because their clothes shed water; but unlike the women just mentioned, they did not carry their day's provisions in a basket, but they carryed in their hands or hid under their clothing as best they might, the morsel of bread which must serve them as food until time for them to return home.

Thus to the strain of an insufferably long

* Note that this was before the era of railroads and street cars. (Translator.)

day— at feast fifteen hours—is added for these wretehes the fatigue of the painful daily journeys. Consequently they reach home overwhelmed by the need of sleep, and next day they rise before they are completely rested in order to reach the factory by the opening time."

Now, look at the holes in which were packed those who lodge in the town: "I saw at Mulhouse in Dornach, and the neighboring houses, some of those miserable lodgings where two families slept each in its corner on straw thrown on the floor and kept in its place by two planks. ....This wretchedness among the laborers of the cotton industry in the department of the upper Rhine is so extreme that it produces this sad result, that while in the families of the manufacturers, merchants, shop-keepers or factory superintendents, half of the children reach their twenty-first year, this same half ceases to exist before the lapse of two years in the families of weavers and cotton spinners."

Speaking of the labor of the workshop, Villermé adds: "It is not a work, a task, it is a torture and it is inflicted on children of six to eight years. It is this long torture day after day which wastes away the laborers in the cotton spinning factories". And as to the duration of the work Villermé observes, that the convicts in prisons work but ten hours, the slaves in the west Indies work but nine hours, while there existed in France after its Revolution of 1789, which had proclaimed the pompous Rights of Man "factories where the day was sixteen hours, out of which the laborers were allowed only an hour and a half for meals."*

What a miserable abortion of the revolutionary principles of the bourgeoisie! What woeful gifts from its god Progress! The philanthropists hail as benefactors of humanity those who having done nothing to become rich, give work to the poor. Far better were it to scatter pestilence and to poisen the springs than to erect a capitalist factory in the midst of a rural population. Introduce factory work, and farewell joy, health and liberty; farewell to all that makes life beautiful and worth living.†

And the economists go on repeating to the

* L. R. Villermé. "Tableau de l'état physique et moral des ouvriers dans les fabriques de coton, de laine et de soie (1840). It is not because Dollfus, Koechlin and other Alsacian manufacturers were republicans, patriots and protestant philanthropists that they treated their laborers in this way, for Blanqui, the academician, Reybaud, the prototype of Jerome Paturot, and Jules Simon, have observed the same amenities for the working class among the very catholic and monarchical manufacturers of Lille and Lyons. These are capitalist virtues which harmonize delightfuly with all political and religious convictions.

† The Indians of the warlike tribes of Brazil kill their invalids and old people; they show their affection for them by putting an end to a life which is no longer enlivened by combats, feasts and dances. All

laborers, "Work, to increase social wealth", and nevertheless an economist, Destutt de Tracy, answers: "It is in poor nations that people are comfortable, in rich nations they are ordinarily poor"; and his disciple Cherbuliez continues: "The laborers themselves in co-operating toward the accumulation of productive capital contribute to the event which sooner or later must deprive them of a part of their wages". But deafened and stupified by their own howlings, the economists answer: "Work, always work, to create your prosperity", and in the name of Christian meekness a priest of the Anglican Church, the Rev. Mr. Townshend, intones: Work, work, night and day. By working you make your poverty increase and your poverty releases us from imposing work upon you by force of law. The legal imposition of work "gives too much trouble, requires too much violence and makes too much noise. Hunger, on the contrary, is not only a pressure which is peaceful, silent and incessant, but as it is the most natural motive for work and industry, it

---

primitive peoples have given these proofs of affection to their relatives: the Massagetae of the Caspian Sea (Herodotus), as well as the Wens of Germany and the Celts of Gaul. In the churches of Sweden even lately they preserved clubs called family clubs which served to deliver parents from the sorrows of old age. How degenerate are the modern proletarians to accept with patience the terrible miseries of factory labor!

also provokes to the most powerful efforts." Work, work, proletarians, to increase social wealth and your individual poverty; work, work, in order that becoming poorer, you may have more reason to work and become miserable. Such is the inexorable law of capitalist production.

Because, lending ear to the fallacious words of the economists, the proletarians have given themselves up body and soul to the vice of work, they precipitate the whole of society into these industrial crises of over-production which convulse the social organism. Then because there is a plethora of merchandise and a dearth of purchasers, the shops are closed and hunger scourges the working people with its whip of a thousand lashes. The proletarians, brutalized by the dogma of work, not understanding that the over-work which they have inflicted upon themselves during the time of pretended prosperity is the cause of their present misery, do not run to the granaries of wheat and cry: "We are hungry, we wish to eat. True we have not a red cent, but beggars as we are, it is we, nevertheless, who harvested the wheat and gathered the grapes." They do not besiege the warehouse of Bonnet, or Jujurieux, the inventor of industrial convents, and cry out: "M. Bonnet, here are your working women, silk workers, spinners, weavers; they are shivering pitifully under their patched cotton dresses, yet it is they who have spun and woven the silk robes of the fashionable women of all Christendom. The poor creatures working thirteen hours a day, had no time to think of their toilet. Now, they are out of work and have time to rustle in the silks they have made. Ever since they lost their milk teeth they have devoted themselves to your fortune and have lived in abstinence. Now they are at leisure and wish to enjoy a little of the fruits of their labor. Come, M. Bonnet, give them your silks, M. Harmel shall furnish his muslins, M. Pouyer-Quertier his calicos, M. Pinet his boots for their dear little feet, cold and damp. Clad from top to toe and gleeful, they will be delightful to look at. Come, no evasions, you are a friend of humanity, are you not, and a Christian into the bargain? Put at the disposal of your working girls the fortune they have built up for you out of their flesh; you want to help business, get your goods into circulation,—here are consumers ready at hand. Give them unlimited credit. You are simply compelled to give credit to merchants whom you do not know from Adam or Eve, who have given you nothing, not even a glass of water. Your working women will pay the debt the best they can. If at maturity they let their notes go to protest, and if they have nothing to attach, you can demand that they pay you in prayers. They will send you to paradise better than your black-gowned priests steeped in tobacco."

Instead of taking advantage of periods of crisis, for a general distribution of their products and a universal holiday, the laborers, perishing with hunger, go and beat their heads against the doors of the workshops. With pale faces, emaciated bodies, pitiful speeches they assail the manufacturers: "Good M. Chagot, sweet M. Schneider, give us work, it is not hunger, but the passion for work which torments us". And these wretches, who have scarcely the strength to stand upright, sell twelve and fourteen hours of work twice as cheap as when they had bread on the table. And the philanthropists of industry profit by their lockouts to manufacture at lower cost.

If industrial crises follow periods of overwork as inevitably as night follows day, bringing after them lockouts and poverty without end, they also lead to inevitable bankruptcy. So long as the manufacturer has credit he gives free rein to the rage for work. He borrows, and borrows again, to furnish raw material to his laborers, and goes on producing without considering that the market is becoming satiated and that if his goods don't happen to be sold, his notes will still come due. At his wits' end, he implores the banker, he throws himself at his feet, offering his blood, his honor. "A little gold will do my business better", answers the Rothschild. "You have 20,000 pairs of hose in your warehouse; they are worth 20c. I will take them at 4c." The banker gets possession of the goods and sells them at 6c or 8c, and pockets certain frisky dollars which owe nothing to anybody: but the manufacturer has stepped back for a better leap. At last the crash comes and the warehouses disgorge. Then so much merchandise is thrown out of the window that you cannot imagine how it came in by the door. Hundreds of millions are required to figure the value of the goods that are destroyed. In the last century they were burned or thrown into the water.*

But before reaching this decision, the manufacturers travel the world over in search of markets for the goods which are heaping up. They force their government to annex Congo,

* At the Industrial Congress held in Berlin in Jan. 21, 1879, the losses in the iron industry of Germany during the last crisis were estimated at $109,056,000.

to seize on Tonquin, to batter down the Chinese Wall with cannon shots to make an outlet for their cotton goods. In previous centuries it was a duel to the death between France and England as to which should have the exclusive privilege of selling to America and the Indies. Thousands of young and vigorous men reddened the seas with their blood during the colonial wars of the sixteenth, seventeenth and eighteenth centuries.

There is a surplus of capital as well as of goods. The financiers no longer know where to place it. Then they go among the happy nations who are loafing in the sun smoking cigarettes and they lay down railroads, erect factories and import the curse of work. And this exportation of French capital ends one fine morning in diplomatic complications. In Egypt, for example, France, England and Germany were on the point of hairpulling to decide which usurers shall be paid first. Or it ends with wars like that in Mexico where French soldiers are sent to play the part of constables to collect bad debts.*

---

* M. Clemenceau's "Justice" said on April 6, 1880, in its financial department: "We have heard this opinion maintained: that even without pressure the billions of the war of 1870 would have been equally lost for France, that is under the form of loans periodically put out to balance the budgets of foreign coun-

These individual and social miseries, however great and innumerable they may be, however eternal they appear, will vanish like hyenas and jackals at the approach of the lion, when the proletariat shall say "I will". But to arrive at the realization of its strength the proletariat must trample under foot the prejudices of Christian ethics, economic ethics and free-thought ethics. It must return to its natural instincts, it must proclaim the Rights of Laziness, a thousand times more noble and more sacred than the anaemic Rights of Man concocted by the metaphysical lawyers of the bourgeois revolution. It must accustom itself to working but three hours a day, reserving the rest of the day and night for leisure and feasting.

Thus far my task has been easy; I have had but to describe real evils well known, alas, by all of us; but to convince the proletariat that the ethics innoculated into it is wicked, that the unbridled work to which it has given itself up for the last hundred years is the most terrible

---

tries; this is also our opinion." The loss of English capital on loans of South American Republics is estimated at a billion dollars. The French laborers not only produced the billion dollars paid Bismarck, but they continued to pay interest on the war indemnity to Ollivier, Girardin, Bazaine and other income drawers, who brought on the war and the rout. Nevertheless they still have one shred of consolation: these billions will not bring on a war of reprisal.

scourge that has ever struck humanity, that work will become a mere condiment to the pleasures of idleness, a beneficial exercise to the human organism, a passion useful to the social organism only when wisely regulated and limited to a maximum of three hours a day; this is an arduous task beyond my strength. Only communist physiologists, hygienists and economists could undertake it. In the following pages I shall merely try to show that given the modern means of production and their unlimited reproductive power it is necessary to curb the extravagant passion of the laborers for work and to oblige them to consume the goods which they produce.

III.

THE CONSEQUENCES OF OVER-PRODUCTION.

A Greek poet of Cicero's time, Antiparos, thus sang of the invention of the water-mill (for grinding grain), which was to free the slave women and bring back the Golden Age: "Spare the arm which turns the mill, O, millers, and sleep peacefully. Let the cock warn you in vain that day is breaking. Demeter has imposed upon the nymphs the labor of the slaves, and behold them leaping merrily over the wheel, and behold the axle tree, shaken, turning with its spokes and making the heavy rolling stone revolve. Let us live the life of our fathers, and let us rejoice in idleness over the gifts that the goddess grants us." Alas!, the leisure which the pagan poet announced has not come. The blind, perverse and murderous passion for work transforms the liberating machine into an instrument for the enslavement of free men. Its productiveness impoverishes them.

A good workingwoman makes with her needles only five meshes a minute, while certain circular knitting machines make 30,000 in the same time. Every minute of the machine is thus equivalent to a hundred hours of the workingwomen's labor, or again, every minute of the machine's labor, gives the workingwomen ten days of rest. What is true for the knitting industry is more or less true for all industries reconstructed by modern machinery. But what do we see? In proportion as the machine is improved and performs man's work with an ever increasing rapidity and exactness, the laborer, instead of prolonging his former rest times, redoubles his ardor, as if he wished to rival the machine. O, absurd and murderous competition!

That the competition of man and the machine

might have free course, the proletarians have abolished wise laws which limited the labor of the artisans of the ancient guilds; they have suppressed the holidays.* Because the producers of that time worked but five days out of seven, are we to believe the stories told by lying economists, that they lived on nothing but air and fresh water? Not so, they had leisure to taste the joys of earth, to make love and to frolic, to banquet joyously in honor of the jovial god of idleness. Gloomy England, immersed in protestantism, was then called "Merrie Eng-

* Under the old regime, the laws of the church guaranteed the laborer ninety rest days, fifty-two Sundays and thirty-eight holidays, during which he was strictly forbidden to work. This was the great crime of catholicism, the principal cause of the irreligion of the industrial and commercial bourgeoisie: under the revolution, when once it was in the saddle, it abolished the holidays and replaced the week of seven days by that of ten, in order that the people might no longer have more than one rest day out of the ten. It emancipated the laborers from the yoke of the church in order the better to subjugate them under the yoke of work.

The hatred against the holidays does not appear until the modern industrial and commercial bourgeoisie takes definite form, between the fifteenth and sixteenth centuries. Henry IV asked of the pope that they be reduced. He refused because "one of the current heresies of the day is regarding feasts" (Letters of Cardinal d'Ossat). But in 1666 Perefixus, archbishop of Paris, suppressed seventeen of them in his diocese. Protestantism, which was the Christian religion adapted to the new industrial and commercial needs of the bourgeoisie, was less solicitous for the people's rest. It dethroned the saints in heaven in order to abolish their feast days on earth.

Religious reform and philosophical free thought were but pretexts which permitted the jesuitical and rapacious bourgeoisie to pilfer the feast days of the people.

and." Rabelais, Quevedo, Cervantes, and the unknown authors of the romances make our mouths water with their pictures of those monumental feasts* with which the men of that time regaled themselves between two battles and two devastations, in which everything "went by the barrel". Jordaens and the Flemish School have told the story of these feasts in their delightful pictures. Where, O, where, are the sublime gargantuan stomachs of those days; where are the sublime brains encircling all human thought? We have indeed grown puny and degenerate. Embalmed beef, potatoes, doctored wine and Prussian schnaps, judiciously combined with compulsory labor have weakened our bodies and narrowed our minds. And the times when man cramps his stomach and the machine enlarges its out-put are the very times when the economists preach to us the Malthusian theory,

---

* These gigantic feasts lasted for weeks. Don Rodrigo de Lara wins his bride by expelling the Moors from old Calatrava, and the Romancero relates the story:

Les bodas fueron en Burgos
Las tornabodas en Salas:
En bodas y tornabodas
Pasaron siete semanas
Tantas vienen de las gentes
Que no caben por las plazas

(The wedding was at Bourges. the infaring at Salas. In the wedding and the infaring seven weeks were spent. So many people came that the town could not hold them.......).

The men of these seven-weeks weddings were the heroic soldiers of the wars of independence.

the religion of abstinence and the dogma of work. Really it would be better to pluck out such tongues and throw them to the dogs.

Because the working class, with its simple good faith, has allowed itself to be thus indoctrinated, because with its native impetuosity it has blindly hurled itself into work and abstinence, the capitalist class has found itself condemned to laziness and forced enjoyment, to unproductiveness and overconsumption. But if the over-work of the laborer bruises his flesh and tortures his nerves, it is also fertile in griefs for the capitalist.

The abstinence to which the productive class condemns itself obliges the capitalists to devote themselves to the over-consumption of the products turned out so riotously by the laborers. At the beginning of capitalist production a century or two ago, the capitalist was a steady man of reasonable and peaceable habits. He contented himself with one wife or thereabouts. He drank only when he was thirsty and ate only when he was hungry. He left to the lords and ladies of the court the noble virtues of debauchery. Today every son of the newly rich makes it incumbent upon himself to cultivate the disease for which quicksilver is a specific in order to justify the labors imposed upon the workmen in quicksilver mines; every capitalist crams himself with capons stuffed with truffles and with the choicest brands of wine in order to encourage the breeders of blooded poultry and the growers of Bordelais. In this occupation the organism rapidly becomes shattered, the hair falls out, the gums shrink away from the teeth, the body becomes deformed, the stomach obtrudes abnormally, respiration becomes difficult, the motions become labored, the joints become stiff, the fingers knotted. Others, too feeble in body to endure the fatigues of debauchery, but endowed with the bump of philanthropic discrimination, dry up their brains over political economy, or juridical philosophy in elaborating thick soporific books to employ the leisure hours of compositors and pressmen. The women of fashion live a life of martyrdom, in trying on and showing off the fairy-like toilets which the seamstresses die in making. They shift like shuttles from morning until night from one gown into another. For hours together they give up their hollow heads to the artists in hair, who at any cost insist on assuaging their passion for the construction of false chignons. Bound in their corsets, pinched in their boots, decollette to make a coal-miner blush, they whirl around the whole night through at their charity balls in order to pick up a few cents for poor people,—sanctified souls!

To fulfill his double social function of non-producer and over-consumer, the capitalist was not only obliged to violate his modest taste, to lose his laborious habits of two centuries ago and to give himself up to unbounded luxury, spicy indigestibles and syphilitic debauches, but also to withdraw from productive labor an enormous mass of men in order to enlist them as his assistants.

Here are a few figures to prove how colossal is this waste of productive forces. According to the census of 1861, the population of England and Wales comprised 20,066,244 persons, 9,776,259 male and 10,289,965 female. If we deduct those too old or too young to work, the unproductive women, boys and girls, then the "ideological professions", such as governors, policemen, clergy, magistrates, soldiers, prostitutes, artists, scientists, etc., next the people exclusively occupied with eating the labor of others under the form of land-rent, interest, dividends, etc.... there remains a total of eight million individuals of both sexes and of every age, including the capitalists who function in production, commerce, finance, etc. Out of these eight millions the figures run:

Agricultural laborers, including herdsmen, servants and farmers' daughters living at home 1,098,261
Factory Workers in cotton, wool, hemp, linen silk, knitting................ 642,607
Mine Workers 565,835
Metal Workers (blast furnaces, rolling mills, etc.) 396,998
Domestics 1,208,648

"If we add together the textile workers and the miners, we obtain the figures of 1,208,442; if to the former we add the metal workers, we have a total of 1,039,605 persons; that is to say, in each case a number below that of the modern domestic slaves. Behold the magnificent result of the capitalist exploitation of machines."* To this class of domestics, the size of which indicates the stage attained by capitalist civilization, must still be added the enormous class of unfortunates devoted exclusively to satisfying the vain and expensive tastes of the rich classes: diamond cutters, lace-makers, embroiderers, binders of luxurious books, seamstresses employed on expensive gowns decorators of villas, etc.†

---

* Karl Marx's "Capital".

† "The proportion in which the population of the country is employed as domestics in the service of the wealthy class indicates its progress in national wealth

Once settled down into absolute laziness and demoralized by enforced enjoyment, the capitalist class in spite of the injury involved in its new kind of life, adapted itself to it. Soon it began to look upon any change with horror. The sight of the miserable conditions of life resignedly accepted by the working class and the sight of the organic degradation engendered by the depraved passion for work increased its aversion for all compulsory labor and all restrictions of its pleasures. It is precisely at that time that, without taking into account the demoralization which the capitalist class had imposed upon itself as a social duty, the proletarians took it into their heads to inflict work on the capitalists Artless as they were, they took seriously the theories of work proclaimed by the economists and moralists, and girded up their loins to inflict the practice of these theories upon the capitalists. The proletariat hoisted the banner, "He who will not work Neither shall he Eat". Lyons in 1831 rose up for bullets or work. The federated laborers of March 1871 called their

---

and civilization." (R. M. Martin, "Ireland Before and After the Union," 1818). Gambetta, who has denied that there was a social question ever since he ceased to be the poverty stricken lawyer of the Café Procope, undoubtedly alluded to this ever-increasing domestic class when he announced the advent of new social strata.

uprising "The Revolution of Work". To these outbreaks of barbarous fury destructive of all capitalist joy and laziness, the capitalists had no other answer than ferocious repression, but they know that if they have been able to repress these revolutionary explosions, they have not drowned in the blood of these gigantic massacres the absurd idea of the proletariat wishing to inflict work upon the idle and reputable classes, and it is to avert this misfortune that they surround themselves with guards, policemen, magistrates and jailors, supported in laborious unprodutiveness. There is no more room for illusion as to the function of modern armies. They are permanently maintained only to suppress the "enemy within". Thus the forts of Paris and Lyons have not been built to defend the city against the foreigner, but to crush it in case of revolt. And if an unanswerable example be called for, we mention the army of Belgium, that paradise of capitalism. Its neutrality is guaranteed by the European powers, and nevertheless its army is one of the strongest in proportion to its population. The glorious battlefields of the brave Belgian army are the plains of the Borinage and of Charleroi. It is in the blood of the unarmed miners and laborers that the Belgian officers temper their swords and win their epaulets. The nations of Europe have not national armies but mercenary armies. They protect the capitalists against the popular fury which would condemn them to ten hours of mining or spinning. Again, while compressing its own stomach the working class has developed abnormally the stomach of the capitalist class, condemned to over-consumption.

For alleviation of its painful labor the capitalist class has withdrawn from the working class a mass of men far superior to those still devoted to useful production and has condemned them in their turn to unproductiveness and over-consumption. But this troop of useless mouths in spite of its insatiable voracity, does not suffice to consume all the goods which the laborers, brutalized by the dogma of work, produce like madmen, without wishing to consume them and without even thinking whether people will be found to consume them.

Confronted with this double madness of the laborers killing themselves with over-production and vegetating in abstinence, the great problem of capitalist production is no longer to find producers and to multiply their powers but to discover consumers, to excite their appetites and create in them fictitious needs. Since the European laborers, shivering with cold and hunger, refuse to wear the stuffs they weave, to drink the wines from the vineyards they tend, the poor manufacturers in their goodness of heart must run to the ends of the earth to find people to wear the clothes and drink the wines: Europe exports every year goods amounting to billions of dollars to the four corners of the earth, to nations that have no need of them.* But the explored continents are no longer vast enough. Virgin countries are needed. European manufacturers dream night and day of Africa, of a lake in the Saharan desert, of a railroad to the Soudan. They anxiously follow the progress of Livingston, Stanley, Du Chaillu; they listen open-mouthed to the marvelous tales of these brave travelers. What unknown wonders are contained in the "dark continent"! Fields are sown with elephants' teeth, rivers of cocoanut oil are dotted with gold, millions of backsides, as bare as the faces of Dufaure and Girardin, are awaiting cotton goods to teach them dec-

* Two examples: The English government to satisfy the peasants of India, who in spite of the periodical famines desolating their country insist on cultivating poppies instead of rice or wheat, has been obliged to undertake bloody wars in order to impose upon the Chinese Government the free entry of Indian opium. The savages of Polynesia, in spite of the mortality resulting from it are obliged to clothe themselves in the English fashion in order to consume the products of the Scotch distilleries and the Manchester cotton mills.

ency, and bottles of schnaps and bibles from which they may learn the virtues of civilization.

But all to no purpose: the over-fed capitalist, the servant class greater in numbers than the productive class, the foreign and barbarous nations, gorged with European goods; nothing, nothing can melt away the mountains of products heaped up higher and more enormous than the pyramids of Egypt. The productiveness of European laborers defies all consumption, all waste.

The manufacturers have lost their bearings and know not which way to turn. They can no longer find the raw material to satisfy the lawless depraved passion of their laborers for work. In our woolen districts dirty and half rotten rags are raveled out to use in making certain cloths sold under the name of renaissance, which have about the same durability as the promises made to voters. At Lyons, instead of leaving the silk fiber in its natural simplicity and suppleness, it is loaded down with mineral salts, which while increasing its weight, make it friable and far from durable. All our products are adulterated to aid in their sale and shorten their life. Our epoch will be called the "Age of adulteration" just as the first epochs of humanity received the names of "The Age of Stone", "The

Age of Bronze", from the character of their production. Certain ignorant people accuse our pious manufacturers of fraud, while in reality the thought which animates them is to furnish work to their laborers, who cannot resign themselves to living with their arms folded. These adulterations, whose sole motive is a humanitarian sentiment, but which bring splendid profits to the manufacturers who practice them, if they are disastrous for the quality of the goods, if they are an inexhaustible source of waste in human labor, nevertheless prove the ingenuous philanthropy of the capitalists, and the horrible perversion of the laborers, who to gratify their vice for work oblige the manufacturers to stifle the cries of their conscience and to violate even the laws of commercial honesty.

And nevertheless, in spite of the overproduction of goods, in spite of the adulterations in manufacturing, the laborers encumber the market in countless numbers imploring: Work! Work! Their superabundance ought to compel them to bridle their passion; on the contrary it carries it to the point of paroxysm. Let a chance for work present itself, thither they rush; then they demand twelve, fourteen hours to glut their appetite for work, and the next day they are again thrown out on the pavement with no more food for their vice. Every year in all industries lockouts occur with the regularity of the seasons. Over-work, destructive of the organism, is succeeded by absolute rest during two or four months, and when work ceases the pittance ceases. Since the vice of work is diabolically attached to the heart of the laborers, since its requirements stifle all the other instincts of nature, since the quantity of work required by society is necessarily limited by consumption and by the supply of raw materials, why devour in six months the work of a whole year; why not distribute it uniformly over the twelve months and force every workingman to content himself with six or five hours a day throughout the year instead of getting indigestion from twelve hours during six months? Once assured of their daily portion of work, the laborers will no longer be jealous of each other, no longer fight to snatch away work from each other's hands and bread from each other's mouths, and then, not exhausted in body and mind, they will begin to practice the virtues of laziness.

Brutalized by their vice, the laborers have been unable to rise to the conception of this fact, that to have work for all it is necessary to apportion it like water on a ship in distress. Meanwhile certain manufacturers in the name of capitalist exploitation have for a long time demanded a legal limitation of the work day. Before the commission of 1860 on professional education, one of the greatest manufacturers of Alsace, M. Bourcart of Guebwiller, declared: "The day of twelve hours is excessive and ought to be reduced to eleven, while work ought to be stopped at two o'clock on Saturday. I advise the adoption of this measure, although it may appear onerous at first sight. We have tried it in our industrial establishments for four years and find ourselves the better for it, while the average production, far from having diminished, has increased." In his study of machines M. F. Passy quotes the following letter from a great Belgian manufacturer M. Ottevaere: "Our machines, although the same as those of the English spinning mills, do not produce what they ought to produce or what those same machines would produce in England, although the spinners there work two hours a day less. We all work two good hours too much. I am convinced that if we worked only eleven hours instead of thirteen we should have the same product and we should consequently produce more ecconomically." Again, M. Leroy Beaulieu affirms that it is a remark of a great Belgian manufacturer that the weeks in which a holiday falls result in a product not less than ordinary weeks.*

An aristocratic government has dared to do what a people, duped in their simplicity by the moralists, never dared. Despising the lofty and moral industrial considerations of the economists, who like the birds of ill omen, croaked that to reduce by one hour the work in factories was to decree the ruin of English industry, the government of England has forbidden by a law strictly enforced to work more than ten hours a day, and as before England remains the first industrial nation of the world.†

The experiment tried on so great a scale is on record; the experience of certain intelligent capitalists is on record. They prove beyond a doubt that to strengthen human production it is necessary to reduce the hours of labor and multiply the pay days and feast days, yet the French nation is not convinced. But if the miserable reduction of two hours has increased English production by almost one-third in ten years, what breathless speed would be given to French pro-

* Paul Leroy-Beaulieu. La Question Ouvrière au XIX siècle, 1872.

† It should be observed that this was written in 1883, since which time the United States has taken the first rank. The soundness of Lafargue's reasoning is confirmed by the fact that in this country the hours of labor in the most important industries are even less than in England. (Translator.)

duction by a legal limitation of the working day to three hours. Cannot the laborers understand that by over-working themselves they exhaust their own strength and that of their progeny, that they are used up and long before their time come to be incapable of any work at all, that absorbed and brutalized by this single vice they are no longer men but pieces of men, that they kill within themselves all beautiful faculties, to leave nothing alive and flourishing except the furious madness for work. Like Arcàdian parrots, they repeat the lesson of the economist: "Let us work, let us work to increase the national wealth.' O, idiots, it is because you work too much that the industrial equipment develops slowly. Stop braying and listen to an economist, no other than M. L. Reybaud, whom we were fortunate enough to lose a few months ago. "It is in general by the conditions of hand-work that the revolution in methods of labor is regulated. As long as hand-work furnishes its services at a low price, it is lavished, while efforts are made to economize it when its services become more costly." *

To force the capitalists to improve their machines of wood and iron it is necessary to raise wages and diminish the working hours of the

* Louis Reybaud. Le coton, son regime, ses problèmes (1863).

machines of flesh and blood. Do you ask for proofs? They can be furnished by the hundreds. In spinning, the self-acting mule was invented and applied at Manchester because the spinners refused to work such long hours as before. In America the machine is invading all branches of farm production, from the making of butter to the weeding of wheat. Why, because the American, free and lazy, would prefer a thousand deaths to the bovine life of the French peasant. Plowing, so painful and and so crippling to the laborer in our glorious France, is in the American West an agreeable open-air pastime, which he practices in a sitting posture, smoking his pipe nonchalantly.

IV.

NEW SONGS TO NEW MUSIC.

We have seen that by diminishing the hours of labor new mechanical forces will be conquered for social production. Furthermore, by obliging the laborers to consume their products the army of workers will be immensely increased. The capitalist class once relieved from its function of universal consumer will hasten to dismiss its train of soldiers, magistrates, journalists, procurers, which it has withdrawn from useful labor to help it in consuming and wasting. Then the labor market will overflow. Then will be required an iron law to put a limit on work. It will be impossible to find employment for that swarm of former unproductives, more numerous than insect parasites, and after them must be considered all those who provide for their needs and their vain and expensive tastes. When there are no more lackeys and generals to decorate, no more free and married prostitutes to be covered with laces, no more cannons to bore, no more palaces to build, there will be need of severe laws to compel the working women and workingmen who have been employed on embroidered laces, iron workings, buildings, to take the hygienic and calisthenic exercises requisite to re-establish their health and improve their race. When once we begin to consume European products at home instead of sending them to the devil, it will be necessary that the sailors, dock handlers and the draymen sit down and learn to twirl their thumbs. The happy Polynesians may then love as they like without fearing the civilized Venus and the sermons of European moralists.

And that is not all: In order to find work for all the non-producers of our present society, in order to leave room for the industrial equipment to go on developing indefinitely, the working class will be compelled, like the capitalist class, to do violence to its taste for abstinence and to develop indefinitely its consuming capacities. Instead of eating an ounce or two of gristly meat once a day, when it eats any, it will eat juicy beefsteaks of a pound or two; instead of drinking moderately of bad wine, it will become more orthodox than the pope and will drink broad and deep bumpers of Bordeaux and Burgundy without commercial baptism and will leave water to the beasts.

The proletarians have taken into their heads to inflict upon the capitalists ten hours of forge and factory; that is their great mistake, because of social antagonisms and civil wars. Work ought to be forbidden and not imposed. The Rothschilds and other capitalists should be allowed to bring testimony to the fact that throughout their whole lives they have been perfect vagabonds, and if they swear they wish to continue to live as perfect vagabonds in spite of the general mania for work, they should be pensioned and should receive every morning at the city hall a five-dollar gold piece for their pocket money. Social discords will vanish. Bond holders and capitalists will be first to rally to the popular party, once convinced that far from wishing them harm, its purpose is rather to relieve them of the labor of over-consumption and waste, with which they have been overwhelmed since their birth. As for the capitalists who are incapable of proving their title to the name of vagabond, they will be allowed to follow their instincts. There are plenty of disgusting occupations in which to place them. Dufaure might be set at cleaning public closets, Gallifet* might perform surgical operations on diseased horses and hogs. The members of the amnesty commission might be sent to the stock yards to pick out the oxen and the sheep to be slaughtered. The senators might play the part of undertakers and lackeys in funeral processions. As for the others, occupations could be found for them on a level with their intelligence. Lorgeril and Broglie could cork champagne bottles, only they would have to be muzzled as a precaution against intoxication. Ferry, Freycinet and Tirard might destroy the bugs and vermin in the departments of state and other public houses. It would, however, be necessary to put the public funds out of the reach of the capitalists out of due regard for their acquired habits.

But vengeance, harsh and prolonged, will be

---

* Gallifet was the general who was directly responsible for the massacre of thousands of French workingmen at the closing days of the Paris Commune.

heaped upon the moralists who have perverted nature, the bigots, the canters, the hypocrites, "and other such sects of men who disguise themselves like maskers to deceive the world. For whilst they give the common people to understand that they are busied about nothing but contemplation and devotion in fastings and maceration of their sensuality,—and that only to sustain and aliment the small fraility of their humanity,—it is so far otherwise that on the contrary, God knows, what cheer they make; et *Curios simulant, sed Bacchanalia vivunt.** You may read it in great letters, in the coloring of their red snouts, and gulching bellies as big as a tun, unless it be when they perfume themselves with sulphur."† On the days of great popular rejoicing, when instead of swallowing dust as on the 15th of August and 14th of July under capitalism, the communists and collectivists will eat, drink and dance to their hearts' content, the members of the Academy, of moral and political sciences, the priests with long robes and short, of the economic, catholic, protestant, jewish, positivist and free-thought church; the propagandists of Malthusianism, and of Christian, altruistic, independent or dependent ethics, clothed in yel-

* They simulate Curius but live like Bacchanals. (Juvenal.)

† Rabelais "Pantagruel," Book II, Chapter XXXIV, Translation of Urquhart and Motteux.

low, shall be compelled to hold a candle until it burns their fingers, shall starve in sight of tables loaded with meats, fruits and flowers and shall agonize with thirst in sight of flowing hogsheads. Four times a year with the changing seasons they shall be shut up like the knife grinders' dogs in great wheels and condemned to grind wind for ten hours.

The lawyers and legislators shall suffer the same punishment. Under the regime of idleness, to kill the time, which kills us second by second, there will be shows and theatrical performances always and always. And here we have the very work for our bourgeois legislators. We shall organize them into traveling companies to go to the fairs and villages, giving legislative exhibitions. The generals in riding boots, their breasts brilliantly decorated with medals and crosses, shall go through the streets and courts levying recruits among the good people. Gambetta and his comrade Cassagnac shall tend door. Cassagnac, in full duelist costume, rolling his eyes and twisting his mustache, spitting out burning tow, shall threaten every one with his father's pistol* and sink into a hole as soon as they show

* Paul de Cassagnac, like his father, Granier, was prominent as a conservative politician, journalist and duelist.

him Lullier's portrait. Gambetta will discourse on foreign politics and on little Greece, who makes a doctor of him and would set Europe on fire to pilfer Turkey; on great Russia that stultifies him with the mincemeat she promises to make of Prussia and who would fain see mischief brewing in the west of Europe so as to feather her nest in the east and to strangle nihilism at home; on Mr. Bismark who was good enough to allow him to pronounce himself on the amnesty ..... then uncovering his mountainous belly smeared over with red and white and blue, the three national colors, he will beat the tattoo on it, and enumerate the delicate little ortolans, the truffles and the glasses of Margaux and Y'quem that it has gulped down to encourage agriculture, and to keep his electors of Belleville in good spirits.

In the barracks the entertainment will open with the "Electoral Farce."

In the presence of the voters with wooden heads and asses' ears, the bourgeois candidates, dressed as clowns, will dance the dance of political liberties, wiping themselves fore and aft with their freely promising electoral programs, and talking with tears in their eyes of the miseries of the people and with copper in their voices of the glories of France. Then the heads of the voters will bray solidly in chorus, hi han! hi han!

Then will start the great play, "The Theft of the Nation's Goods."

Capitalist France, an enormous female, hairy-faced and bald-headed, fat, flabby, puffy and pale, with sunken eyes, sleepy and yawning, is stretching herself out on a velvet couch. At her feet Industrial Capitalism, a gigantic organism of iron, with an ape-like mask, is mechanically devouring men, women and children, whose thrilling and heart-rending cries fill the air; the bank with a marten's muzzle, a hyena's body and harpy—hands, is nimbly flipping coins out of his pocket. Hordes of miserable, emaciated proletarians in rags, escorted by gendarmes with drawn sabers, pursued by furies lashing them with whips of hunger, are bringing to the feet of capitalist France heaps of merchandise, casks of wine, sacks of gold and wheat. Langlois, his nether garment in one hand, the testament of Proudhon in the other and the book of the national budget between his teeth, is encamped at the head of the defenders of national property and is mounting guard. When the laborers, beaten with gun stocks and pricked with bayonets, have laid down their burdens, they are driven away and the door is opened to the manufacturers, merchants and bankers. They hurl themselves pell mell upon the heap, devouring cotton goods, sacks of wheat, ingots of gold, emptying casks of wine. When they have devoured all they can, they sink down, filthy and disgusting objects in their ordure and vomitings. Then the thunder bursts forth, the earth shakes and opens, Historic Destiny arises, with her iron foot she crushes the heads of the capitalists, hiccoughing, staggering, falling, unable to flee. With her broad hand she overthrows capitalist France, astounded and sweating with fear.

* * *

If, uprooting from its heart the vice which dominates it and degrades its nature, the working class were to arise in its terrible strength, not to demand the Rights of Man, which are but the rights of capitalist exploitation, not to demand the Right to Work which is but the right to misery, but to forge a brazen law forbidding any man to work more than three hours a day, the earth, the old earth, trembling with joy would feel a new universe leaping within her. But how should we ask a proletariat corrupted by capitalist ethics, to take a manly resolution....

Like Christ, the doleful personification of ancient slavery, the men, the women and the children of the proletariat have been climbing painfully for a century up the hard Calvary of pain;

for a century compulsory toil has broken their bones, bruised their flesh, tortured their nerves; for a century hunger has torn their entrails and their brains. O Laziness, have pity on our long misery! O Laziness, mother of the arts and noble virtues, be thou the balm of human anguish!

APPENDIX

Our moralists are very modest people. If they invented the dogma of work, they still have doubts of its efficacy in tranquilizing the soul, rejoicing the spirit, and maintaining the proper functioning of the entrails and other organs. They wish to try its workings on the populace, *in anima vili,* before turning it against the capitalists, to excuse and authorize whose vices is their peculiar mission.

But, you, three-for-a-cent philosophers, why thus cudgel your brains to work out an ethics the practice of which you dare not counsel to your masters? Your dogma of work, of which you are so proud, do you wish to see it scoffed at, dishonored? Let us open the history of ancient peoples and the writings of their philosophers and law givers. "I could not affirm," says the father of history, Herodotus, "whether the Greeks derived from the Egyptians the contempt which they have for work, because I find the same contempt established among the Thracians, the Cythians, the Persians, the Lydians; in a word, because among most barbarians, those who learn mechanical arts and even their children are regarded as the meanest of their citizens. All the Greeks have been nurtured in this principle, particularly the Lacedaemonians." *

"At Athens the citizens were veritable nobles who had to concern themselves but with the defense and the administration of the community, like the savage warriors from whom they descended. Since they must thus have all their time free to watch over the interests of the republic, with their mental and bodily strength, they laid all labor upon the slaves. Likewise at Lacedaemon, even the women were not allowed to spin or weave that they might not detract from their nobility." †

The Romans recognized but two noble and free professions, agriculture and arms. All the citizens by right lived at the expense of the treasury without being constrained to provide for their living by any of the sordid arts (thus, they designated the trades), which rightfully belonged

---

* Herodotus, Book II.
† Biot. De L'abolition de L'esclavage ancien en Occident, 1840.

to slaves. The elder Brutus to arouse the people, accused Tarquin, the tyrant, of the special outrage of having converted free citizens into artisans and masons.*

The ancient philosophers had their disputes upon the origin of ideas but they agreed when it came to the abhorrence of work. "Nature," said Plato in his social utopia, his model republic, "Nature has made no shoemaker nor smith. Such occupations degrade the people who exercise them. Vile mercenaries, nameless wretches, who are by their very condition excluded from political rights. As for the merchants accustomed to lying and deceiving, they will be allowed in the city only as a necessary evil. The citizen who shall have degraded himself by the commerce of the shop shall be prosecuted for this offense. If he is convicted, he shall be condemned to a year in prison; the punishment shall be doubled for each repeated offense." †

In his "Economics," Xenophon writes, "The people who give themselves up to manual labor are never promoted to public offices, and with good reason. The greater part of them, condemned to be seated the whole day long, some even to endure the heat of the fire continually,

* Livy, Book I.
† Plato's "Republic," Book V.

cannot fail to be changed in body, and it is almost inevitable that the mind be affected." "What honorable thing can come out of a shop?" asks Cicero. "What can commerce produce in the way of honor? Everything called shop is unworthy an honorable man. Merchants can gain no profit without lying, and what is more shameful than falsehood? Again, we must regard as something base and vile the trade of those who sell their toil and industry, for whoever gives his labor for money sells himself and puts himself in the rank of slaves."*

Proletarians, brutalized by the dogma of work, listen to the voice of these philosophers, which has been concealed from you with jealous care: A citizen who gives his labor for money degrades himself to the rank of slaves, he commits a crime which deserves years of imprisonment.

Christian hypocrisy and capitalist utilitarianism had not perverted these philosophers of the ancient republics. Speaking for free men, they expressed their thought naively. Plato, Aristotle, those intellectual giants, beside whom our latter day philosophers are but pygmies, wish the citizens of their ideal republics to live in the most complete leisure, for as Xenophon observed,

* Cicero's "De Officiis." I. 42.

"Work takes all the time and with it one has no leisure for the republic and his friends." According to Plutarch, the great claim of Lycurgus, wisest of men, to the admiration of posterity, was that he had granted leisure to the citizens of Sparta by forbidding to them any trade whatever. But our moralists of Christianity and capitalism will answer, "These thinkers and philosophers praised the institution of slavery." Perfectly true, but could it have been otherwise, granted the economic and political conditions of their epoch? War was the normal state of ancient societies. The free man was obliged to devote his time to discussing the affairs of state and watching over its defense. The trades were then too primitive and clumsy for those practicing them to exercise their birth-right of soldier and citizen; thus the philosophers and law-givers, if they wished to have warriors and citizens in their heroic republics, were obliged to tolerate slaves. But do not the moralists and economists of capitalism praise wage labor, the modern slavery; and to what men does the capitalist slavery give leisure? To people like Rothschild, Schneider, and Madame Boucicaut, useless and harmful slaves of their vices and of their domestic servants. "The prejudice of slavery dominated the minds of Pythagoras and Aristotle,"—this has been written disdainfully; and yet Aristotle foresaw: that if every tool could by itself execute its proper function, as the masterpieces of Daedalus moved themselves or as the tripods of Vulcan set themselves spontaneously at their sacred work; if for example the shuttles of the weavers did their own weaving, the foreman of the workshop would have no more need of helpers, nor the master of slaves."

Aristotle's dream is our reality. Our machines, with breath of fire, with limbs of unwearying steel, with fruitfulness, wonderful inexhaustible, accomplish by themselves with docility their sacred labor. And nevertheless the genius of the great philosophers of capitalism remains dominated by the prejudice of the wage system, worst of slaveries. They do not yet understand that the machine is the saviour of humanity, the god who shall redeem man from the sordidae artes and from working for hire, the god who shall give him leisure and liberty.

SOCIALISM
AND THE INTELLECTUALS

ADDRESS DELIVERED AT PARIS MARCH 23, 1900, AT A MEETING CALLED BY THE GROUP OF COLLECTIVIST STUDENTS ATTACHED TO THE PARTI OUVRIER FRANÇAIS.

Ladies and Gentlemen:—I am happy to deliver this address under the presidency of Vaillant, because it is a pledge of the close and lasting union between our two organizations, and because Vaillant is one of the intellectuals of the socialist party; he is acknowledged to be the most learned of French socialists and perhaps of European socialists, now that Marx, Engels and Lavroff are no longer with us.

The group of collectivist students which has organized this conference, has been led to choose this subject, because French socialism has just passed through a crisis which is not exactly one of growth, though such it has been called, but which has been caused by the arrival of a certain number of bourgeois intellectuals within the ranks of the party. It is therefore interesting to examine the situation of the intellectuals in capitalist society, their historic role since the revolution of 1789, and the manner in which the bourgeoisie has kept the promises it made them when it was struggling against the aristocracy.

The eighteenth century was the century of reason—everything, religion, philosophy, science, politics, privileges of classes, of the state, of municipalities, was submitted to its pitiless criticism. Never in history has there been such a fermentation of ideas and such a revolutionary preparation of men's minds. Mirabeau, who himself played a great role in the ideological agitation, might well say in the national assembly: "We have no time to think, but happily, we have a supply of ideas." All that was needed was to realize them. Capitalism, to reward the intellectuals who had labored with so much enthusiasm for the coming of its revolution, promised them honors and favors; intelligence and wisdom, as well as virtue, should be the sole privileges of the society it was founding upon the ruins of the old order. Promises cost it little; it announced to all men that it brought them joy and happiness, with liberty, equality and fraternity, which, although eternal principles, were now born for the first time. Its social world was to be so new that even before the Republic was proclaimed, Camille Desmoulins demanded that they begin a new era which should date from the taking of the Bastile.

I need not teach you what application capitalism has made of these eternal principles which by way of cynical raillery, the Republic carves on the lintels of her prisons, her penitentiaries, her barracks and her halls of state.* I will only remind you that savage and barbarous tribes, uncorrupted by civilization, living under the regime of common property, without inscribing anywhere these eternal principles, without even formulating them, practice them in a manner more perfect than ever was dreamed of by the capitalists who discovered them in 1789.

It did not take long to determine the value of the promises of capitalism; the very day it opened its political shop, it commenced proceedings in bankruptcy. The constituent assembly, which formulated the Rights of man and of the citizen and proclaimed equality before the law, discussed and voted, in 1790, an electoral act

* Ever since the French Revolution the law has required the words "Liberté, Egalité, Fraternité, to be placed over the door of every public building in France.—Translator.

which established inequality before the law; no one was to be a voter but the "active citizen," paying in money a direct tax equal to three days' labor, and no one was to be eligible to office but the citizen paying a direct tax of a "silver mark," about 55 francs. "But under the law of the silver mark," clamored Loustalot, Desmoulins and the intellectualists without real estate, "Jean Jacques Rousseau, whose 'Social Contract is the bible of the revolution, would be capable neither of voting nor of holding office." The electoral law deprived so many citizens of political rights, that in the municipal elections of 1790, at Paris, a city which counted about half a million inhabitants, there were but 12,000 voters, Bailly was chosen mayor by 10,000 votes.

If the eternal principles were not new, it is also true that the flattering promises made by the intellectuals had already begun to be realized before the advent of capitalism to power. The church, which is a theocratic democracy, opens her bosom to all. That they may enter, all lay aside their titles and privileges, and all can aspire to the highest positions; popes have risen from the lower ranks of society. Sixtus Fifth had in his youth tended swine. The church of the middle ages jealously attracted to herself the thinkers and men of learning, although she respected the preference of those who wished to remain laymen, but extended over them her protection and her favors; she allowed them all boldness of thought, on the single condition of keeping up the appearance of faith, and never leaving her enclosure to lavish themselves upon the vulgar. Thus Copernicus might write and dedicate to the pope his "treatise on the revolutions of the celestial bodies," in which, contrary to the teaching of the Bible, he proves that the earth turns around the sun. But Copernicus was a canon at Frannbourg and he wrote in Latin. When a century later Galileo, who was not identified with the clergy and who on the contrary sought the protection of the secular authorities, professed publicly, at Venice and Florence, the theories of Copernicus, the Vatican stretched out its terrible hand over him and forced the illustrious old man to deny his scientific belief. Even after the crisis of Protestantism, the church preserved its liberality toward the scientists who belonged to it. Mersenne, a monk of the order of the Minimes, one of the great geometers of the seventeenth century, a precursor and friend of Descartes, corresponded freely with Hobbes, the father of modern materialism: the notes of the French edition of "De Cive" contain fragments of this correspondence.

The church, in keeping up this liberal conduct, may have been animated by a disinterested love of pure science, but what chiefly concerned her was the interest of her dominancy; she wished to monopolize the intellectuals and science, just is in the old theocratic Egypt the priests had done to whom the Greek thinkers resorted in search of the first elements of science and philosophy.

It would be insulting capitalism to attribute to it a disinterested love of science, which from its point of view has but one reason for existence, that of utilizing natural forces to the enhancement of its wealth. It cares nothing for pure speculation and it is by way of self-defence that it allows its scientists to devote their mental energy to theoretic researches instead of exhausting it on practical applications. This contempt for pure speculation is shown under a philosophic form in the positivism of Auguste Comte, who embodies so well the narrowness of the groveling spirit of capitalism.

But if science apart from its industrial applications does not interest the bourgeoisie their solicitude for the intellectuals takes on none of the forms which we saw in that of the church.

and nowhere is their indifference to them better shown than in the relative position of material property and of intellectual property before the law.

Material property, whatever its origin, is by capitalist law a thing eternal; it is forever assured to its possessor; it is handed down from father to son to the end of the centuries, and no civil or political power may lay upon it a sacrilegious hand. We have lately seen a characteristic example of this inviolability of material property.

The keeper of the signal station at Durban transmitted to the Boers heliographic dispatches informing them regarding the ships which entered the harbor, the men, the horses and the munitions of war which they transported. His treason brought him 125,000 francs, which, like an intelligent capitalist, he deposited in the bank. The English military authorities seized the traitor, condemned him and shot him, but they respected his property so honorably acquired, and his widow and son are now its legitimate possessors. The law, apart from certain variations, being the same in all capitalist countries, things go on in France as in England. No authority could lay hand on the property of Bazaine, nor make De Lesseps, Cottu and their families disgorge the millions artfully extracted from the "lambs" on Panama canal stock.

This legal sanctity of property is a new thing, in France it dates from the revolution of 1789. The old regime, which had small respect for this sort of property, authorized the confiscation of the property of those legally condemned, and the abolition of confiscation is one of the first reforms demanded in the petitions of Paris and several provincial cities to the states general. Capitalism, by forbidding the confiscation of property obtained by fraudulent and infamous means, proclaims that the source of its fortune is quite as fraudulent and infamous as that of criminals and traitors.

Capitalist law has none of these amenities for intellectual property. Literary and artistic property such as the law protects at all has but a precarious life, limited to the life of the author and a certain time after his death—fifty years according to the latest legislation; that time passed, it lapses into common property; for example, beginning with March of this year, any publisher has the right to bring out for his own profit the works of Balzac, the genius of romantic literature.

Literary property, though a matter of interest to publishers, who are certainly few in number, brings no benefit to the mass of the capitalist class, but not so with property in inventions, which is of prime importance to all the manufacturing and mercantile capitalists. Consequently over it the law extends no protection. The inventor, if he wishes to defend his intellectual property against capitalist pirates, must begin by buying that right, taking out a patent, which he must renew every year; on the day he misses a payment, his intellectual property becomes the lawful prey of the robbers of capitalism. Even if he pays, he can secure that right only for a time; in France, fourteen years. And during these few years, not long enough generally to get his invention fully introduced into practical industry, it is he, the inventor, who at his own expense has to set in motion the machinery of the law against the capitalist pirates who rob him.

The trade-mark, which is a capitalistic property that never required any intellectual effort, is on the contrary indefinitely protected by law like material property.

It is with reluctance that the capitalist class has granted the inventor the right of defending his intellectual property, for by virtue of its position as the ruling class it regards itself as entitled to the fruits of intellectual labor as well as of manual labor; just as the feudal lord asserted his right of possession over the property of his serfs. The history of the inventors of our century is the monstrous story of their spoliation by the capitalists; it is a long and melancholy roll of martyrs. The inventor, by the very fact of his genius, is condemned with his family to ruin and suffering.

It is not only inventions requiring long and laborious study, heavy outlay for their completion and long time for their introduction, that plunge the inventor into the inferno of poverty; this is equally true of inventions that are most simple, most immediately applicable and most fertile in rich results. I will mentiton but one example: there lately died at Paris in extreme poverty a man whose invention saves millions of francs a year to the railroads and mining companies; he had discovered a way to utilize the mountains of coal dust that encumbered the neighborhood of wharfs and mines by converting it into "briquettes," such as are today in common use for fuel.

The capitalist bourgeoisie, the most revolutionary class that ever oppressed human societies, cannot increase its wealth without continuously revolutionizing the means of production, continuously incorporating into its industrial equipment new applications of mechanics, chemistry and physics. Its thirst for inventions is so insatiable that it creates factories for inventions. Certain American capitalists united in constructing for Edison at Menlo Park the most wonderful laboratory in the world, and in putting at his disposal trained scientists, chosen workmen, and the ordinary materials necessary to make and keep on making inventions which the capitalists patent, exploit or sell. Edison, who is himself a shrewd business man, has taken care to secure for himself a part of the benefits brought by the Menlo Park inventions.

But not all inventors are able like Edison to dictate terms to the capitalists who equip invention factories. The Thompson-Houston Company at Paris and Siemens at London and Berlin,* in connection with their plants for turning out electrical machinery, have laboratories where ingenious men are kept busy searching out new applications of electricity. At Frankfort the manufactory of aniline dyes, the largest in the world, where anti-pyrine, that mineral quinine, was discovered, keeps on its pay roll more than a hundred chemists to discover new products of coal-

* It is a well-known fact that in the American establishments of these and similar companies each workman before receiving employment must sign papers transferring to the corporation the title to all inventions made by him while in its service.—Translator.

tar. Each discovery is at once patented by the house, which, by way of encouragement, gives a reward to the inventor.

We may up to a certain point regard all factories and workshops as laboratories for inventions, since a considerable number of improvements in machinery have been devised by workmen in the course of their work. The inventor having no money to patent and apply his discovery, the employer takes out the patent in his own name, and in accordance with the spirit of capitalist justice, it is he who reaps all the benefit. When the government takes it into its head to rewards talent, it is the employer who receives the decoration; the inventive workman, who is not an intellectual, continues to revolve like the other machines under the black and greasy number which distinguishes him, and as in this capitalist world he must be content with little, he consoles himself for his poverty by the reflection that his invention is bringing wealth and honor to his employer.

The capitalist class, which to increase its wealth is in pressing need of inventions, is in even more imperative need of intellectuals to supervise their application and to direct its industrial machinery. The capitalists, before they equipped invention factories, had organized factories to turn out intellectuals. Dollfus, Scherer-Kestner and other employes of Alsace, the most intelligent, most philanthropic and consequently the heaviest exploiters in France before the war, had founded with their spare pennies at Mulhouse, schools of design, of chemistry and of physics, where the brightest children of their workmen were instructed gratis, in order that they might always have at hand and at reasonable figure the intellectual capacities required for carrying on their industries. Twenty years ago the directors of the Mulhouse school persuaded the municipal council of Paris to establish the city school of chemistry and physics. At the beginning, whether it is still the case I do not know, the pupils were recruited in the common schools, they received a higher education, gratis, a dinner at noon at the school, and fifty francs a month to indemnify the parents for the loss from the fact that their sons were not in the workshop.

On the platform of the constituent assembly of 1790 the Marquis of Foucault could declare that to be a laborer it was not necessary to know how to read and write. The necessities of industrial production compel the capitalist of to-day to speak in language altogether different; his economic interests and not his love of humanity and of science force him to encourage and to develop both elementary and higher education.

But the slave merchants of ancient Rome were, by the same title, patrons of education. To the more intelligent of their human merchandise they gave instruction in medicine, philosophy, Greek literature, music, science, etc. The education of the slave enhanced his market value. The slave who was an expert cook brought a better figure than the slave doctor, philosopher or literator. In our days it is still so; the big capitalists pay their chief cooks better than the state pays the professors of liberal arts, even though they be members of the Institute. But contrary to the practice of the Roman slave merchants, our capitalist class lavishes instruction only in order to depress the selling price of intellectual capacity.

Greek mythology tells how Midas had the gift of turning everything into gold; the capitalist class has a similar property, it transforms everything that it touches into merchandise; it has done this for intellectual capacities; chemists, engineers and Latin scholars are bought like she-asses and guano.

A voice: "And they buy deputies, too!"

People who have no tallow nor veal nor socks

to sell have their conscience and their votes; when they are deputies, they are bought.

When intellectual capacities become merchandise they have to be treated like other merchandise, and they are. When there are many oysters in the market the price of oysters goes down, but when the arrivals are scarce the price goes up. When chemists and engineers are plenty on the labor market, the price of inventors and of chemists goes down. Now that the Central School and the School of Physics and Chemistry turn out yearly upon the pavements of Paris chemists by the dozen, their price has considerably gone down. Twenty years ago the capitalist paid a chemist reasonably, he gave him $100 to $120 a month and engaged him by the year. The employers whose regard for an employee is measured by what they have to pay him, were full of politeness and consideration for their chemists who cost so dear. But since they have been abundant, their price has fallen to $40 and $30 a month; in the north they are not engaged by the year but for the sugar season, which lasts three or four months, at the end of which they are discharged with the workmen. Go and shift for yourself, says the employer. Next fall when the beets come I know I shall find chemists to superintend making them into sugar.

The chemists are not exceptional; you know only too well that in all branches there is an overproduction of intellectuals, and that when a place is vacant, tens and hundreds offer themselves to fill it; and it is this pressure which permits the capitalists to lower the price of the intellectuals and to put it even below the wage of the manual laborer.

Poverty is harder for the intellectual than for the workingman; it bruises him morally and physically. The workingman, enduring hardships from childhood and knocking about the street and the shops, is accustomed to enduring the troubles of life; the intellectual, brought up in a hot-house, has the life bleached out of him by the shadow of the college walls, his nervous system is over-developed and takes on an unhealthy impressionability. What the workingman endures thoughtlessly is to him a painful shock. The intellectual is wounded to the depths of his moral being by the exigencies of a wage-worker's life. With the same or even a higher wage the intellectual is in a worse economic condition than the laborer, for the latter may dress as cheaply as he likes, but the former, if only not to offend the eye of his employer and his chiefs with whom he is brought in contact is obliged to dress expensively and even elegantly. He must save on his food what he has to spend on his clothing.

The capitalists have degraded the intellectuals below the economic level of the manual laborers. This is their reward for having so magnificently prepared the way for the bourgeois revolution of the eighteenth century.

Jaures in his preface to the Socialist History of France says that "the intellectual bourgeoisie, offended by a brutal and commercial society and disenchanted with the bourgeois power, is rallying to the support of socialism." Unfortunately nothing could be less exact. This transformation of the intellectual faculties into merchandise, which ought to have filled the intellectuals with wrath and indignation, leaves them indifferent. Never would the free citizen of the ancient republics of Athens and Rome have submitted to such degradation. The free man who sells his work, says Cicero, lowers himself to the rank of the slaves. Socrates and Plato were indignant against the Sophists who required pay for their philosophic teaching, for to Socrates and Plato thought was too noble a thing to be bought and sold like carrots and shoes. Even the French clergy of 1789 resented as a mortal insult the proposition to pay a salary for worship. But our intellectuals are accustoming themselves to such degradation.

Spurred on by the mercantile passion, they are never better satisfied with themselves or with society than when they succeed in selling their intellectual merchandise at a good price; they have even come to the point of making its selling price the measure of its value. Zola, who is one of the most distinguished representatives of literary intellectualism, estimates the artistic value of a novel by the number of editions sold. To sell their intellectual merchandise has become in them such an all-absorbing principle that if one speaks to them of socialism, before they inquire into its theories, they ask whether in the socialistic society intellectual labor will be paid for and whether it will be rewarded equally with manual labor.

Imbeciles! they have eyes but they see not that it is the capitalist bourgeoisie which establishes that degrading equality; and to increase its wealth degrades intellectual labor to the point of paying it at a lower rate than manual labor.

We should have to put off the triumph of socialism not to the year 2,000 but to the end of the world if we had to wait upon the delicate, shrinking and impressionable hesitancy of the intellectuals. The history of the century is at hand to teach us just how much we have a right to expect from these gentlemen.

Since 1789 governments of the most diverse and opposed character have succeeded each other in France; and always, without hesitation, the intellectuals have hastened to offer their devoted services. I am not merely speaking of those two-for-a-cent intellectuals who litter up the newspapers, the parliaments and the economic associations; but I mean the scientists, the university professors, the members of the Institute; the higher they raise their heads, the lower they bow the knee.

Princes of science, who ought to have conversed on equal terms with kings and emperors, have marketed their glory to buy offices and favors from ephemeral ministers. Cuvier, one of the mightiest geniuses of the modern era, whom the revolution took from the household of a nobleman to make of him at twenty-five years one of the Museum professors, Cuvier took the oath of allegiance and served with fidelity the Republic, Napoleon, Louis XVIII, Charles X and Louis Philippe, the last of whom created him a peer of France to reward him for his career of servility.

To devote one's self to all governments without distinction is not enough. Pasteur placed his glorious name at the service of the financiers, who placed him in the administrative council of the Credit Foncier, side by side with Jules Simon, with dukes and counts, with senators, deputies and ex-ministers, in order to entrap the "lambs." When De Lesseps was equipping his colossal swindle of the Panama canal, he enrolled the intellectuals of the Institute, of the French Academy, of literature, of the clergy, of all the circles of higher life.

It is not in the circle of the intellectuals, degraded by centuries of capitalist oppression, that we must seek examples of civic courage and moral dignity. They have not even the sense of professional class-consciousness. At the time of the Dreyfus affair, a certain minister discharged, as if he had been a mere prison guard, one of the professors of chemistry in the Polytechnic school who had had the rare courage to give public expression to his opinion. When in a factory the employer dismisses a workman in too arbitrary a fashion, his comrades grumble, and sometimes quit work, even though misery and hunger await them in the street.

All his colleagues in the Polytechnic school bowed their heads in silence; each one crouched in self-regarding fear, and what is still more characteristic, not a single partisan of Dreyfus in the Society of the Rights of Man or in the ranks of the press raised a voice to remind them of the idea of professional solidarity. The intellectuals, who on all occasions display their transcendental ethics, have still a long road to travel before they reach the moral plane of the working class and of the socialist party.

The scientists have not only sold themselves to the governments and the financiers; they have also sold science itself to the capitalist-bourgeoisie. When in the eighteenth century there was need to prepare the minds of men for the revolution, by sapping the ideologic foundations of aristocratic society, then science fulfilled its sublime mission of freedom; it was revolutionary; it furiously attacked Christianity and the intuitional philosophy. But when the victorious bourgeoisie decided to base its new power on religion, it commanded its scientists, its philosophers and its men of letters to raise up what they had overthrown; they responded to the need with enthusiasm. They reconstructed what they had demolished; they proved by scientific, sentimental and romantic argument the existence of God the father, of Jesus the son and of Mary the virgin mother. I do not believe history offers a spectacle equal to that presented in the first years of the nineteenth century by the philosophers, the scientists and the literary men, who from revolutionaries and materialists suddenly transformed themselves into reactionaries, intuitionalists and Catholics.

This backward movement still continues; when Darwin published his Origin of Species, which took away from God his role of creator in the organic world, as Franklin had despoiled him of his thunderbolt, we saw the scientists, big and little, university professors and members of the Institute, enrolling themselves under the orders of Flourens, who for his own part had at least his eighty years for an excuse, that they might demolish the Darwinian theory, which was displeasing to the government and hurtful to religious beliefs. The intellectuals exhibited that painful spectacle in the fatherland of Lamark and of Geoffroy Saint-Hilaire, the creators of the evolution theory, which Darwin completed and made proof against criticism.

Today, now that the clerical anxiety is somewhat appeased, the scientists venture to profess the evolution theory, which they never opposed without a protest from their scientific conscience, but they turn it against socialism so as to keep in the good graces of the capitalists. Herbert Spencer, Haeckel and the greatest men in the school of Darwinism demonstrate that the classification of individuals into rich and poor, idlers and laborers, capitalists and wage-earners, is the necessary result of the inevitable laws of nature, instead of being the fulfillment of the will and the justice of God. Natural selection, they say, which has differentiated the organs of the human body, has forever fixed the ranks and the functions of the social body. They have, through servility, even lost the logical spirit. They are indignant against Aristotle because he, being unable to conceive of the abolition of slavery, declared that the slave was marked off by nature; but they fail to see that they are saying something equally monstrous when they affirm that natural selection assigns to each one his place in society.

Thus it is no longer God or religion which condemn the workers to wretchedness—it is science. Never was there an intellectual bankruptcy more fraudulent.

M. Brunetieres, one of those intellectuals who do not feel their degradation and who joyfully fulfill their servile task, was right when he proclaimed the failure of science. He does not suspect how colossal this bankruptcy is.

Science, the great emancipator, that has tamed the powers of nature, and might in so doing have freed man from toil to allow him to develop freely his faculties of mind and body; science, become the slave of capital, has done nothing but supply means for capitalists to increase their wealth, and to intensify their exploitation of the working class. Its most wonderful applications to industrial technique have brought to the children, the women and the men of the working class nothing but overwork and misery!

The middle-class revolutionary party of 1789 cried out in horror and indignation against the lords, who through the long summer nights compelled their serfs to beat the ponds near their castles in order to keep the frogs from croaking. What would they say if they saw what we see? Improvements in lighting date from the capitalist period. At the end of the last century Argant and Carcel invented the lamp with a double current of air, at the beginning of this Chevreul invented the stearic candle, then gas was discovered, then petroleum, then the electric light, turning night into day. What benefits have these scientific improvements in lighting brought to the workers? They have enabled employers to impose night work upon millions of proletarians, not in the midsummer nights and in the balmy air of the fields, but through nights of summer and winter in the poisonous air of the workshops and factories. The industrial applications of mechanics and chemistry have transformed the happy and stimulating work of the artisan into a torture which exhausts and kills the proletarian.

When science subdued the forces of nature to the service of man, ought she not to have given leisure to the workers that they might develop themselves physically and intellectually; ought she not to have changed the "vale of tears" into a dwelling place of peace and joy? I ask you, has not science failed in her mission of emancipation?

The obtuse capitalist himself is conscious of this failure; so he directs his economists and his other intellectual domestics to prove to the working class that it has never been so happy and that its lot goes on improving.

The economists, considering that to deserve the good graces of the capitalists it was not enough to falsify economic facts, are suppressing economic science, which is becoming dangerous for the domination of capital. Ever since Adam Smith and Ricardo they go on repeating the same errors regarding value, regarding the productivity of the predatory and idle capitalist, compiling facts and arranging statistics which guide the capitalists in their speculations; but they dare not draw conclusions and build systems with the materials that they have accumulated. When Ricardo wrote, the phenomena of modern production were beginning their evolution, their communist tendencies could not be perceived, one could then study them without taking sides and could build up a science without fear of wounding the interests of capital. But now that they have arrived at their full development and show clearly their communal tendencies, the economists shut their eyes that they may not see, and they wage war against the principles established by Ricardo, which after having served as a basis for the old bourgeois economy, have become the points of departure of the Marxian economy. To take a whack at the socialist theories and put themselves at the service of the financiers, like barkers and fakirs of their bogus goods, are the intellectual functions of the economists. Latterly the owners of silver mines have enlisted them to sing the praises of bimetallism, while Cecil Rhodes, Barnato, Beit, Robbers & Company called them in to boom the Transvaal gold mines.

The intellectuals of art and literature, like the jesters of the old feudal courts, are the entertainers of the class which pays them. To satisfy the tastes of the capitalists and beguile their leisure—this is their sole artistic aim. The men of letters are so well broken to this servile duty that they do not understand the spirit of Moliere, their great ancestor, all the while that they adore the letter of his works. Moliere is the writer most written about in France; learned men have devoted themselves to gathering up the scattered fragments of his erratic and careless youth, to fixing the date and the hour of the representations of his comedies; if they had unearthed an authentic piece of excrement from him they would have set it in gold and would kiss it devotedly, but the spirit of Moliere escapes them. You have read, as I have, many critical analyses of his dramas. Did you ever find one of them which brought out in clear light the role of this militant playwright, who more than a century before Beaumarchais and before revolution, at Versailles, in the very court of the great monarch, thrust at the nobility of the court and of the provinces, attacked the church before which Descartes and the rest trembled, hurled his jests at Aristotle, the unquestioned authority of La Sorbonne, that secular church; who ridiculed the Pyrrhonism which the neo-Kantians of our own days oppose to the materialist philosophy of Marxian socialism, but which then was the weapon of the Catholics, of Pascal, of Huet, the bishop of Avranches, to strike and to overthrow human reason, with its impudent desire or reaching knowledge by its own strength. Pitiful, wretched reason, clamored these Kantians before Kant, you can know nothing without the aid of faith! Moliere is unique in European litterature, you must go back to the epoch of glorious Athens to find his counterpart in Aristophanes.

If the bourgeois critics timidly and unintelligently mention this side of Moliere, there is another of which their ignorance is complete. Moliere was the man of his class, the champion of the bourgeois class. Like the socialists who say to the workers, "Break with the liberal bourgeoisie, which deceives you when it does not slaughter you;" he cried to the Georges Dandins and to the "bourgeois noblemen," "Avoid the nobles like pests; they deceive you, mock you and rob you."

The great capitalist bourgeoisie does not choose to work, either with its hands or its brain; it chooses merely to drink, to eat, to practice lewdness and to look dignified in its beastly and cumbersome luxury; it does not even deign to occupy itself with politics; men like Rothschild, De Lesseps, Vanderbilt, Carnegie, Rockefeller, do not run for office; they find it more economical to buy the deputies than the voters, and more convenient to put their clerks into the ministries than to take part in parliamentary struggles. The big capitalists interest themselves only in the operations of the stock exchange, which afford the delights of gambling; they dignify these by the pompous name of "speculations," — a word formerly reserved for the highest processes of philosophical or mathematical thought. The capitalists are getting themselves replaced in the supervision and management of the great industrial and commercial enterprises by intellectuals, who carry them on, and usually are well paid for doing so. These intellectuals of industry and politics, the privileged portion of the wage class, imagine that they are an integral part of the capitalist class, while they are only its servants; on every occasion they take up its defense against the working class, which finds in them its worst enemies.

Intellectuals of this description can never be led into socialism; their interests are too closely bound up with those of the capitalist class for them to detach themselves and turn against it. But below these favored few there is a swarming and famishing throng of intellectuals whose lot grows worse in proportion to the increase of thier numbers. These intellectuals belong to socialism. They ought to be already in our ranks.

Their education ought to have given them the necessary intelligence to deal with social problems, but it is this very education which obstructs their hearing and keeps them away from socialism. They think their education confers on them a social privilege, that it will permit them to get through the world by themselves, each making his own way in life by crowding out his neighbor or standing on the shoulders of everyone else. They imagine that their poverty is transitory and that they only need a stroke of good luck to transform them into capitalists. Education, they think, is the lucky number in the social lottery, and it will bring them the grand prize. They do not perceive that this ticket given them by the capitalist class is a fraud, that labor, whether manual or intellectual, has no other chance than to earn its daily pittance, that it has nothing to hope for but to be exploited, and that the more capitalism goes on developing, the more do the chances of an individual raising himself out of his class go on diminishing.

And while they build castles in Spain, capital crushes them, as it has crushed the small merchants and the small manufacturers, who thought they, too, with free credit and a little luck, might become first-class capitalists, whose names should be written in the Great Book of the Public Debt.

The intellectuals, in all that has to do with the understanding of the social movement, do not rise above the intellectual level of those little bourgeois who scoffed so fiercely at the bunglers of 1830 and who, after being ruined and merged in the proletariat, none the less continue to detest socialism; to such a degree were their heads perverted by the religion of property. The intellectuals, whose brains are stuffed with all the prejudices of the bourgeois class, are inferior to those little bourgeois of 1830 and 1848 who at least were not afraid of gunpowder; they have not their spirit of combativeness, they are true imbeciles, — if we restore to this word its original Latin meaning of unsuited for war. Without resistance they endure rebuffs and wrongs and they do not think of uniting, of organizing themselves to defend their interests and give battle to capital on the economic field.

The intellectual proletariat as we know it is a recent growth, it has especially developed in the last forty years. When after the amnesty of the condemned of the Commune, we began again the socialist propaganda, believing that it would be easy to draw the intellectuals into the movement we took up our dwelling in their cultured Latin quarter, Guesde taking up his residence in the Rue de la Pitie, Vaillant in the Rue Monge and I in the Boulevard de Port Royal. We became acquainted with hundreds of young men, students of law, of medicines, of the sciences, but you can count on your fingers those whom we brought into the socialist camp. Our ideas attracted them one day, but the next day the wind blew from another quarter and turned their heads.

An honorable merchant of Bordeaux, a prominent member of the municipal council, said in the time of the empire to my father, who was disturbed over my socialism:

"Friend Lafargue, you must let youth take its course; I was a socialist when I studied at Paris, I was connected with the secret societies and I took part in the movement for demanding of Louis Philippe the pardon of Barbes." The young men of our age turn quickly, let them get back to their homes and they develop prominent abdomens and become reactionaries.

We welcomed joyfully the entrance of Jaures into socialism; we thought that the new form which he brought to our propaganda would make it penetrate into circles that we had not been able to touch. He has in fact made a decided impression on the university circle, and we owe it in part to him that the nurslings of the Ecole Normale have ideas regarding the social movement which are a little less absurd and formless than those with which their learning and intelligence have hitherto been contented. Lately, joining forces with the radical politicians who had lost their working-class following, they have invaded the socialist party. Their souls overflow with the purest intentions; if their peaceful habits prevent them from throwing themselves into the conflict, and if their lofty culture forbids them to take their place in the ranks of the comrades, they nevertheless condescend to instruct us in ethics, to polish off our ignorance, to teach us how to think, to offer us such crumbs of science as we may be able to digest, and to direct us; they modestly offer themselves to us as leaders and schoolmasters.

These intellectuals who have spent their youth in the university that they might become experts on exercises, polishers of phrases, philosophers or doctors, imagine one can improvise himself into a master of the socialist theory by attending a single lecture or by the careless reading of a single pamphlet. Naturalists who had felt the need of painful research to learn the habits of mollusks or of the polyps who live in a community on the coral banks, think that they know enough to regulate human societies, and that by keeping their stand on the first steps of the ascending ladder of animal life they can the better discern the human ideal. The philosophers, the moralists, the historians and the politicians have aims equally lofty; they bring an abundant supply of ideas and a new method of action to replace the imperfect theory and tactics which in all capitalist countries have served to build up socialist parties strong in numbers, unity and discipline.

The class struggle is out of fashion, declare these professors of socialism. Can a line of demarcation be drawn between classes? Do not the working people have savings bank accounts of $20, $40 and $100, bringing them 50 cents, $1.50 and $3.00 of interest yearly? Is it not true that the directors and managers of mines, railroads and financial houses are wage-workers, having their functions and duties in the enterprises which they manage for the account of capitalists? The argument is unanswerable, but by the same token there is no vegetable kingdom nor animal kingdom because we can not separate them "with an ax," as it were, for the reason that at their points of contact, vegetables and animals merge into each other. There is no longer any day or any night because the sun does not appear on the horizon at the same moment all over the earth, and because it is day at the antipodes while it is night here.

The concentration of capital? A worn-out tune of 1850. The corporations by their stocks and bonds parcel out property and distribute it among all the citizens. How blinded we were by our sectarianism when we thought that this new form of property, essentially capitalistic, was enabling the financiers to plunge their thieving hands into the smallest purses, to extract the last pieces of silver.

The poverty of the working class! But it is diminishing and soon will disappear through the constant increase of wages, while interest on money is constantly diminishing; some fine day it will descend to zero and the bourgeois will be overjoyed to offer their beloved capital on the altar of socialism. That to-morrow or the day after the capitalist will be forced to work, is the prediction of Mr. Waldeck-Rousseau. And there are intellectuals whose condition grows worse in proportion as capitalism develops, who are stultified by the utterances of the employers to a point where they affirm that the position of wage-workers is improving, and there are intellectuals who assume to possess some knowledge of political economy, who affirm that interest on money is rapidly diminishing. Could these reformers of socialism perchance be ignorant that Adam Smith calculated at the end of the eighteenth century that 3 per cent was the normal interest of capital running no risk, and that the financiers of our own epoch consider that it is still around 3 per cent that the interest rate must fluctuate. If a few years ago this rate seemed to fall below 2½ per cent, it has risen to-day above 3 per cent. Capital is merchandise, like intellectual capacities and carrots; as such it is subject to the fluctuations of supply and demand. It was then more offered than demanded, whereas since the development of the industrial plant of Russia, since the opening of China to European exploitation, etc., the over-supply of capital has been absorbed and its price rises with its scarcity. But the intellectuals have too many trifles to think of and too many harmonious phrases to construct for giving any thought to economic phenomena. They take for sterling truths all the lies of the capitalists, and repeat with pious conviction the old litanies of the orthodox economic church: "There are no classes, wealth is coming to be distributed more and more equitably, the workers are growing richer and those living on incomes are growing poorer, and the capitalist society is the best of all possible societies; these truths shine forth like suns and none but partisans and mystics can deny them."

These intellectuals propose to modify the tactics as well as the theories of the socialist party; they wish to impose upon it a new method of action. It must no longer strive to conquer the public powers by a great struggle, legal or revolutionary as need may be, but let itself be conquered by every ministry of a republican coalition; it is no longer to oppose the socialist party to all the bourgeois parties; what is needed is to put it at the service of the liberal party; we must no longer organize it for the class struggle, but keep it ready for all the compromises of politicians. And to further the triumph of the new method of action, they propose to disorganize the socialist party, to break up its old systems and to demolish the organizations which for twenty years have labored to give the workers a sense of their class interests and to group them in a party of economic and political struggle.

But the intellectuals will lose their labors; thus far they have only succeeded in drawing closer the ties uniting the socialists of the different organizations, and in making themselves ridiculous.

The intellectuals ought to have been the first of all the various groups to revolt against capitalist society, in which they occupy a subordinate position so little in keeping with their hopes and their talents, but they do not even understand it; they have such a confused idea of it that Auguste Comte, Renan, and others more or less distinguished have cherished the dream of reviving for their benefit an aristocracy copied after the model of the Chinese mandarin system. Such an idea is a reflection of past ages in their heads, for nothing is in more absolute opposition with the modern social movement than such pretensions. The intellectuals in previous states of society formed a world outside and above that of production, having charge only of education, of the direction of religious worship, and of the political administration.

The mechanic industry of these societies combine in the same producer, manual labor and intellectual labor; it was for example the same cabinetmaker who designed and executed the piece of furniture, who bought its first material and who even undertook its sale. Capitalist production has divorced two functions which once were indissolubly united; on the one side it puts the manual workers, who become more and more servants of the machine, and on the other the intellectual workers, engineers, chemists, managers, etc. But these two categories of workers, however different and contrary they may be in their education and habits, are welded together, to the point that a capitalist industry can not be carried on without manual laborers any more than without intellectual wage-workers.

United in production, united under the yoke of capitalist exploitation, united they should be also in revolt against the common enemy. The intellectuals, if they understood their own real interests would come in crowds to socialism, not through philanthropy, not through pity for the miseries of the workers, not through affectation and snobbery, but to save themselves, to assure the future welfare of their wives and children, to fulfill their duty to their class. They ought to be ashamed of being left behind in the social battle by their comrades in the manual category. They have many things to teach them, but they have still much to learn from them; the workingmen have a practical sense superior to theirs, and have given proof of an instinctive intuition of the communist tendencies of modern capitalism which is lacking to the intellectuals, who have only been able by a conscious mental effort to arrive at this conception. If only they had understood their own interests, they would long since have turned against the capitalist class the education which it has generously distributed in order better to exploit them; they would have utilized their intellectual capacities, which are enriching their masters, as so many improved weapons to fight capitalism and to conquer the freedom of their class, the wage-working class.

Capitalist production, which has overthrown the old conditions of life and of work, has elaborated new forms, which already can be discerned without supernatural vision, but which to the intellectuals remain sealed under seven seals. One of the leading lights of intellectualism, M. Durkheim, in his book, "The Division of Labor," which made some noise in university circles, can not conceive of society except on the social pattern of ancient Egypt, each laborer remaining, his life through, penned up in one single trade. However, unless one is so unfortunate as to be affected by the hopeless near-sightedness of the Ecole Normale, one can not help seeing that the machine is suppressing trades, one after the other, in a way to let only one survive, that of the machinist, and that when it has finished its revolutionary work which the socialists will complete by revolutionizing capitalist society, the producer of the communist society will plow and sow with the machine to-day, will spin, will turn wood or polish steel to-morrow, and will exercise in turn all the trades to the greater profit of his health and his intelligence.

The industrial applications of mechanics,

chemistry and physics, which, monopolized by capital, oppress the worker, will, when they shall be common property, emancipate man from toil and give him leisure and liberty.

Mechanical production, which under capitalist direction can only buffet the worker back and forth from periods of over-work to periods of enforced idleness, will when developed and regulated by a communist administration, require from the producer, to provide for the normal needs of society, only a maximum day of two or three hours in the workshop, and when this time of necessary social labor is fulfilled he will be able to enjoy freely the physical and intellectual pleasures of life.

The artist then will paint, will sing, will dance, the writer will write, the musician will compose operas, the philosopher will build systems, the chemist will analyze substances not to gain money, to receive a salary, but to deserve applause, to win laurel wreaths, like the conquerors at the Olympic games, but to satisfy their artistic and scientific passion; for one does not drink a glass of champagne or kiss the woman he loves for the benefit of the gallery. The artist and the scientist may then repeat the enthusiastic words of Kepler, that hero of science: "The elector of Saxony with all his wealth can not equal the pleasure I have felt in composing the Mysterium Cosmographicum."

Will not the intellectuals end by hearing the voice of the socialist calling them to the rescue, to emancipate science and art from the capitalist yoke, to liberate thought from the slavery of commercialism?

THE BANKRUPTCY OF CAPITALISM

The nineteenth century was the century of capitalism. Capitalism filled that century to overflowing with its commerce, its industry, its manners, its fashions, its literature, its art, its science, its philosophy, its religion, its politics and its civil code, more universal than the laws imposed by Rome upon the nations of the ancient world. The capitalist movement, starting from England, the United States and France, has shaken the foundations of Europe and of the world. It has forced the old feudal monarchies of Austria and Germany and the barbaric despotism of Russia to put themselves in line; and in these last days it has gone into the extreme East, into Japan, where it has overthrown the feudal system and implanted the industry and the politics of capitalism.

Capitalism has taken possession of our planet;

its fleets bring together the continents which oceans had separated; its railroads, spanning mountains and deserts, furrow the earth; the electric wires, the nervous system of the globe, bind all nations together, and their palpitations reverberate in the great centers of population. Now for the first time there is a contemporary history of the world. Events in Australia, the Transvaal, China, are known in London, Paris, New York, at the moment they are brought about, precisely as if they happened in the outskirts of the city where the news is published.

Civilized nations live off the products of the whole earth. Egypt, India, Louisiana, furnish the cotton, Australia the wool, Japan the silk, China the tea, Brazil the coffee, New Zealand and the United States the meat and grain. The capitalist carries in his stomach and on his back the spoils of the universe.

The study of natural phenomena has undergone an unprecedented, an unheard-of, development. New sciences, geology, chemistry, physics, etc., have arisen. The industrial application of the forces of nature and of the discoveries of science has taken on a still more startling development; some of the geometrical discoveries of the scientists of Alexandria, two thousand years old, have for the first time been utilized.

The production of machine industry can provide for all demand and more. The mechanical application of the forces of nature has increased man's productive forces tenfold, a hundredfold. A few hours' daily labor, furnished by the able-bodied members of the nation, would produce enough to satisfy the material and intellectual needs of all.

But what has come of the colossal and wonderful development of science, industry and commerce in the nineteenth century? Has it made humanity stronger, healthier, happier? Has it given leisure to the producers? Has it brought comfort and contentment to the people?

Never has work been so prolonged, so exhausting, so injurious to man's body and so fatal to his intelligence. Never has the industrial labor which undermines health, shortens life and starves the intellect been so general, been imposed on such ever-growing masses of laborers. The men, women and children of the proletariat are bent under the iron yoke of machine industry. Poverty is their reward when they work, starvation when they lose their jobs.

In former stages of society, famine appeared only when the earth refused her harvests. In capitalist society, famine sits at the hearth of the working class when granaries and cellars burst with the fruits of the earth, and when the market is gorged with the products of industry.

All the toil, all the production, all the suffering of the working class has but served to heighten its physical and mental destitution, to drag it down from poverty into wretchedness.

Capitalism, controlling the means of production and directing the social and political life of a century of science and industry, has become bankrupt. The capitalists have not even proved competent, like the owners of chattel slaves, to guarantee to their toilers the work to provide their miserable livelihood; capitalism massacred them when they dared demand the right to work —a slave's right.*

The capitalist class has also made a failure of itself. It has seized upon the social wealth to enjoy it, and never was the ruling class more incapable of enjoyment. The newly rich, those who have built up their fortunes by accumulating the filchings from labor, live like strangers in the midst of luxury and artistic treasures, with which they surround themselves through a foolish vanity, to pay homage to their millions.

The leading capitalists, the millionaires and

* I allude to the Days of June, 1848. The insurgents demanded the "Right to Work."

billionaires, are sad specimens of the human race, useless and hurtful. The mark of degeneracy is upon them. Their sickly offspring are old at birth. Their organs are sapped with diseases. Exquisite meats and wines load down their tables, but the stomach refuses to digest them; women expert in love perfume their couches with youth and beauty, but their senses are benumbed. They own palatial dwellings in enchanting sites, and they have no eyes, no feeling for joyful nature, with its eternal youth and change. Sated and disgusted with everything, they are followed everywhere by ennui as by their shadows. They yawn at rising and when they go to bed; they yawn at their fests and at their orgies. They began yawning in their mother's womb.

The pessimism which, in the wake of capitalist property, made its appearance in ancient Greece six centuries before Jesus Christ, and which has since formed the foundation of the moral and religious philosophy of the capitalist class, became the leading characteristic of the philosophy of the second half of the nineteenth century. The pessimism of Theognis sprang from the uncertainties and vicissitudes of life in the Greek cities, torn by the perpetual wars between rich and poor; the pessimism of the capitalist is the bitter fruit of satiety, ennui and the impoverishment of the blood.

The capitalist class is falling into its second childhood; its decreptitude appears in its literature, now returning to its starting point. Romantic literature, the literary form proper to the capitalist class, which started out with the romantic Christianity of Chateaubriand, is returning to the same point, after passing through the historical novel and the character novel. (Witness in this country the immense sale of "Ben Hur" and its imitators.—Translator.) Capitalism, which in its virile and combative youth in the eighteenth century had wished to emancipate itself from Christianity, resigns itself in its old age to practices of the grossest superstition.

The capitalist class, bankrupt, old, useless and hurtful, has finished its historic mission; it persists as ruling class only through its acquired momentum. The proletariat of the twentieth century will execute the decree of history; will drive it from its position of social control. Then the stupendous work in science and industry accomplished by civilized humanity, at the price of such toil and suffering, will engender peace and happiness; then will this vale of tears be transformed into an earthly paradise.

THE WOMAN QUESTION

The bourgeois has thought and still thinks that woman ought to remain at home and devote her activity to supervising and directing the housekeeping, caring for her husband, and manufacturing and nourishing children. Even Xenophon, at the time when the bourgeoisie was newly born and was taking its shape in ancient society, traced the main outlines of this ideal of woman. But if through the course of centuries, this ideal may have appeared reasonable, because it corresponded to economic conditions which prevailed, it is no longer anything more than an ideological survival, since these conditions have ceased to exist.

The domestication of woman presupposes that she fulfills in the household certain numerous functions which absorb all her energy; now, the most important and the most exacting of these domestic labors,—the spinning of wool and linen, the cutting and making up of clothing, laundry work, baking, etc.,—are carried on by capitalistic industry. It furthermore presupposes that man by his contribution to the family capital and his earnings provides for the material needs of the family; now, among the comfortable bourgeoisie, marriage is as much an association of capitals* as a union of persons and often the capital contributed by the wife exceeds that of the husband, and in the small bourgeoisie the gains of the father of the family have fallen so low that the children, —girls as well as boys,—are compelled to earn their living in business, railroad offices, banks,

---

* The dowry has played an important role in the history of woman: at the beginning of the patriarchal period the husband buys her from her father, who has to refund her purchase price if for any cause whatever he repudiates her and sends her back to her family; later this purchase price is returned to him and constitutes her dowry, which her relatives are accustomed to double. From the moment when the wife enters into her husband's house with a dowry, she ceases to be a slave whom he may dismiss, sell and kill. The dowry, which in Rome and Athens became a legal charge upon the property of the husband, was, in case of her repudiation or divorce, to be restored to her in preference to any creditor. "No pleasure is derived from the riches which a woman brings into the household," says a fragment of Euripides, "they only serve to render divorce difficult." The comic authors ridiculed the husbands, who in fear of a suit over the dowry, fell into dependence upon the wife. A character in Plautus says to a husband who is talking against his wife, "You accepted the money of her dowry, you sold your authority—imperium." The wealthy Roman matrons carried their insolence to such a point that they did not trust the management of their dowry to their husbands, they gave it over to the stewards, who sometimes fulfilled with them another service, as the evil-speaking Martial states.

Adultery on the part of the wife involved a legal divorce and the restitution of the dowry, but rather than come to this painful extremity, the husbands

teaching, civil service positions, etc., while it often happens that the young wife continues to work outside in order to help out the resources of the housekeeping, when the earnings of the husband do not suffice to cover the expenses.

The daughters and wives of the small bourgeoisie, as well as those of the working class, thus enter into competition with their father, brothers and husband. This economic antagonism, which the bourgeoisie had prevented from developing by confining the wife to the family dwelling, is becoming general and is intensified in proportion as capitalistic production develops; it invades the fields of the liberal professions—

---

preferred to close their eyes to the foibles of their wives; at Rome and at Athens the law had to strike at them in order to recall them to their marital dignity; in China a certain number of bamboo strokes were applied to the soles of their feet. The penalties not being sufficient to encourage the husbands to repudiate their adulterous wives, the law, in order to prop up masculine virtue, permitted those who denounced the infidelity of the wife to retain a part of the dowry; there were then men who married only in prospect of the adultery of the wife. The Roman women evaded the law by having themselves enrolled in the censor's book on the list of prostitutes, to whom it did not apply. The number of matrons inscribed became so considerable that the Senate, under Tiberius passed a decree forbidding "women who had a patrician for a grandfather, husband or father to traffic in their bodies." (Tacitus, Annals II., 85.) Adultery on the part of the wife in the patrician society of antiquity, as well as in the aristocratic society of the eighteenth century, had become so general that it had so to speak entered into the social customs. It was looked upon lightly as a corrective and accompaniment of marriage.

medicine, law, literature, journalism, the sciences, etc.,—where man had reserved for himself a monopoly, which he imagined was to be eternal. The laborers, as is always the case, have been the first to draw the logical consequences of the participation of woman in social production; they have replaced the ideal of the artisan,—the wife who is nothing but a housekeeper,—by a new ideal,—woman as a companion in their economic and political struggles for the raising of wages and the emancipation of labor.

The bourgeois has not yet succeeded in understanding that his ideal is already long since out of date and that it must be remodeled to correspond to the new conditions of the social environment; nevertheless since the first half of the nineteenth century the ladies of the bourgeoisie have begun to protest against their inferior position in the family, so much the more intolerable in that their dowry placed them on a footing of equality with the husband; they rebelled against the domestic slavery and the parsimonious life to which they were condemned, as well as the deprivation of intellectual and material enjoyments which was imposed upon them; the bolder ones went so far as to demand free love and to ally themselves with the utopian sects which preached the emancipation of woman.* The philosophers and the moralists had the simplicity to believe that they would stop the woman movement by opposing to it the sacred interest of the family, which they declared could not survive without the subjection of woman to the labors of the household, the sewing on of shirt buttons, the mending of hose, etc., her duty was to devote herself to these obscure and thankless labors, in order that man might freely unfold and display his brilliant and superior faculties. These same philosophers, who lectured the rebellious ladies on the cult of the family, sang the praises of capitalist industry, which, by forcing the wife away from the domestic hearth and her child's cradle to condemn her to the forced labor of the factory, destroys the working-class family.

The bourgeois ladies laughed at the sermons, equally imbecile and ethical, of these solemn philosophers; they kept on their way and attained the end they set for themselves; like the patrician lady of ancient Rome and the countess of the eighteenth century, they threw off the cares of housekeeping and of the nursing of the child

* The Saint Simon manifesto of 1830 announced that the religion of Saint Simon had come "to put an end to that shameful traffic, that legal prostitution, which under the name of marriage often blesses the monstrous union of self-surrender and egoism, of light and of ignorance, of youth and decrepitude."

upon mercenaries, that they might devote themselves wholly to the toilet, that they might be the most luxuriously arrayed dolls in the capitalist world and in order to make business move. The daughters and wives of American plutocracy have attained the extreme limits of this sort of emancipation; they are transforming their fathers and husbands into accumulators of millions, which they squander madly. Since the toilet does not exhaust the entire activity of the ladies of capitalism, they find amusement in breaking the marriage contract in order to assert their independence and improve the race. The Communist Manifesto remarks that the innumerable divorce suits in which adultery is alleged are indisputable proofs of the respect inspired in the bourgeois of both sexes by the sacred bonds of marriage which the "licentious socialists" talk of loosening.

When the daughters and wives of the small bourgeoisie, obliged to earn their living and to increase the resources of the family, began to invade the stores, the offices, the civil service and the liberal professions, the bourgeois were seized with anxiety for their means of existence already so reduced; feminine competition would reduce them still further. The intellectuals who took up the defense of the males, thought it prudent not to start afresh with the ethical sermons which had miscarried so piteously in the case of the wealthy bourgeois ladies;—they appealed to science; they demonstrated by reasons which were irrefutable and loftily scientific that woman cannot emerge from the occupations of housekeeping without violating the laws of nature and history. They proved to their complete satisfaction that woman is an inferior being, incapable of receiving a higher intellectual education and of furnishing the combination of attention, energy and agility demanded by the professions in which she was entering into competition with man. Her brain, less voluminous, less heavy and less complex than that of man, is a "child's brain." Her less developed muscles have not the strength for attack and for resistance; the bones of her forearm, her pelvis, her femur, and in fact all her osseous, muscular and nervous system do not permit her to undertake more than the routine of the household. Nature designed her in all her organization to be the servant of man, just as the odious god of the Jews and Christians marked out the race of Ham for slavery.

History contributed its startling confirmation of these ultra scientific truths; the philosophers and the historians affirmed that always and everywhere the wife, subordinate to the man, had been shut up in the house, in the woman's apartments; if such had been her lot in the past, such was to be her destiny in the future, was the positive declaration of Auguste Comte, the profoundest of bourgeois philosophers. Lombroso, the illustrious comedian, went him one better: he seriously declared that social statistics proclaimed the inferiority of woman, since the number of female criminals is below that of male criminals; while buried in these figures, he might have added that the statistics of insanity demonstrate the same inferiority. Thus we see that ethics, anatomy, physiology, social statistics and history riveted forever upon woman the chains of domestic servitude..

II.

Bachofen, Morgan and a crowd of anthropologists have revised the opinion of the historians and philosophers upon the role played by woman in the past. They have shown that everywhere the paternal family, which subordinated woman to man, had been preceded by the maternal family, which gave the first place to woman. The Greek language contains the record of her two conditions: while the Spartans, among whom matriarchal customs persisted, still continued to call her *despoina,* the mistress of the house, the sovereign, the other Greeks gave to the wife the name *damar,* the subdued, the vanquished. The Odyssey, in characterizing Nausicaa, says that she is *parthenos admes,* the girl not subdued, that is to say, without a husband, without a master. The modern expression "yoke of marriage" preserves the ancient idea.

Hesiod, in opposition to Homer, who tells only of patriarchal customs, preserves precious recollections of the matriarchal family; he tells us that when it existed man, even if he were a hundred years old, lived with his prudent mother, — he was fed in her house like a great child. (Works and Days, V. 129-130.) It was not the woman who then had the "child's brain," but the man; everything seems in fact to prove that her intelligence was the first to develop. This intellectual superiority caused her to be deified before man in the primitive religions of Egypt, the Indies, Asia and Greece, and caused the first inventions of the arts and trades, with the exception of metal working, to be attributed to goddesses and not to gods. The Muses, originally three in number, were in Greece, even in preference to Apollo, the goddesses of poetry, music and the dance. Isis, "mother of corn ears and lady of bread," and Demeter, lawgiver, had taught the Egyptians and Greeks the tillage of barley and wheat and made them renounce their anthropophagic repasts. The woman appeared to the prepatriarchal man, like the Germans whom Tacitus knew, as having within herself something holy and providential, *aliquid sanctum et providum* (Germania VIII). Her prudence and foresight gave her this divine character. Must we conclude that this intellectual superiority, which manifested itself when the economic environment is rudimentary, is a natural phenomenon?

But, in any case, it may be asserted that the vitality of woman is superior to that of man. The life insurance companies of the United States, England and Holland, which do not base their calculation upon scientific fairy tales of the intellectuals but upon mortality tables, pay woman an annuity below that which they give man, because her probabilities of death are less. Here for example is the annuity paid for a capital of $1,000 by American and Dutch companies:*

	New York.		Holland.	
Age.	Men.	Women.	Men.	Women.
50 years	$ 76.47	$ 69.57	$ 76.80	$ 73.60
60 years	97.24	88.03	98.50	93.50
70 years	134.31	122.48	142.00	136.70
80 years	183.95	168.00	222.70	211.70

* The French companies make no differences between the sexes because they pay very small annuities. La Génerale, the most important one in France, gives for $1.000 at the age of 50 years an annuity of $64.20; at 60 years $80.80; at 70 years $118.50; at 80 years $134.70. Thus it realizes immense profits; its shares which in 1819 were worth 750 francs each were quoted last January at 31,300 francs.

It may be objected that man, leading a more active life, is more subject to accidents, diseases, and other causes of death, and that consequently the prolonged life of woman does not prove the higher vitality of her organism, but the advantages of a life less subject to accident.

The answer to this objection is found in the statistics of the various nations. There is in no country a perfect equilibrium between the number of women and that of men; for 1,000 men there are in Belgium 1,005 women, in France 1,014, in England 1,062, in Scotland 1,071 and in Norway 1,091. Nevertheless in these countries with the feminine preponderance there is an excess of masculine births: of the whole of Western Europe for every 1000 girls there are born from 1,040 to 1,060 boys. If, in spite of this excess of masculine births, more girls survive, it is because the greater mortality of the boys shows the balance in favor of the girls; and this higher mortality cannot be explained by the life of man being more subject to accident, since it is observed at an early age, notably during the first two years. All the diseases of childhood, with the exception of diphtheria and whooping cough, are to a perceptible extent more fatal among boys than among girls; from zero to five years the male sex is particularly frail; at all ages, except between ten and fifteen years, the male mortality is in excess of the female.

The superior vitality of the female sex is also noticeable in the greater ease with which it builds up its organism. M. Iribe, superintendent of the sanitarium of Hendaye, to which are sent Parisian children from three to fourteen years of age, who are afflicted with anaemia, incipient tuberculosis, scrofula and rickets, reports that at the time of their dismissal, at the end of six months, the progress in weight, girth and chest development is incomparably higher in the girls than in the boys, the increase in weight is double and often more.

The same statement has been made by other superintendents of sanitariums. (Bulletin Medical, No. 81, 1903.)

Woman undeniably possesses a greater vitality than man. M. Gustav Loisel has made inquiry "as to whether this difference existed in embryonic life, and what may be its cause?" He has communicated the results of his inquiries to the Biological Society of Paris, which published them in its Bulletin of November 6, 1903.

M. Loisel availed himself of 792 weights and measurements made upon 72 foetuses at the

Maternity Hospital of Paris by C. E. Legou;* from the following weights of the foetuses at three, four, five and six months he obtains the following figures:

	Males.	Females.	Differences.	
	Grammes.		Grammes.	
Total weight	1908.18	1708.11	200.07	in favor of males
Kidneys	16.87	17.19	2.67	in favor of males
Superrenal glands	5.15	6.43	0.32	in favor of females
Liver	88.35	96.31	1.28	in favor of females
Spleen	2.59	2.38	7.90	in favor of females
Thymus	3.89	3.97	0.21	in favor of males
Heart	10.97	12.60	0.08	in favor of females
Lungs	47.29	44.62	1.63	in favor of females
Brain	236.94	235.17	1.17	in favor of males

"These figures thus show us," says M. Loisel, "a preponderance already existing in favor of the females as regards the kidneys, the superrenal glands, the liver, the thymus and the heart; this predominance is the more noticeable since the total weight of the body is larger in the male than in the female."

If now we take the relation between the total weight and the weight of the organs which are heaviest in the male, we find that the proportion is still in favor of the female:

PROPORTION OF TOTAL WEIGHT.

	Males.	Females.
Spleen	1 to 736	1 to 718
Lungs	1 to 40	1 to 38
Brain	1 to 8	1 to 7

* E. Legou. "Some Considerations on the Development of the Foetus." Paris 1903. The weights and measurements of M. Legou were made for official use.

The organs here examined, brain included, are thus absolutely or relatively heavier in the female foetus than in the male foetus.

M. Loisel has also examined into the proportion of the weights of the different organs to the total weight according to the age of the foetus. He has prepared a table, from which I take only the figures concerning the brain:

AGE	TOTAL WEIGHT		Proportion of weight of brain to total weight.	
	Males Grammes	Females Grammes	Males	Females
3 Months	58.33	65.96	1/6.5	1/7
4 Months	167.25	182.58	1/7.3	1/6.6
5 Months	336.33	295.00	1/7.6	1/7.5
6 Months	732.58	636.00	1/8:3	1/7.3

The weight of the male foetus, which is below that of the female foetus, at three months, when the sex has just been determined, grows more rapidly and the proportion between the weight is always to the advantage of the females from the fourth month on.

"To sum up," says M. Loisel, "all the organs are heavier in the female foetus than in the male foetus up to about the fourth month. The predominance then passes over to the male, but only for the lungs and the organs for sex-union, thus the cardiac muscle always remains heavier in the female. The organs which are of real service to the individual during the embryonic life always remain more developed in the female sex.

"If now we consider that the differences in favor of the females are especially in the liver, the heart, the superrenal glands and the kidneys, we shall come to the conclusion that the greater vitality of the female organisms corresponds to their being better nourished and better purified."*

III.

The superior organization possessed by woman at birth, assuring her throughout her life a much greater vitality, is probably demanded by the part she plays in the production of the species, a part altogether more prolonged and exhausting than that of the man who, when fertilization is accomplished, has no more to do, while then the travail of woman begins, to continue during long months, through pregnancy and after birth. The women of savage tribes suckle their children for two years and more. It sometimes happens

* The latest observations upon ants and bees tend to prove that the fertilized eggs would give birth to females and to workers; and the nonfertilized to males, which consequently would be born from eggs that are less complex.

that the male pays dear for his inutility; after union, the bees kill the males, and the male spider must hastily take himself off that he may not be devoured by the larger and stronger female. Among the Sakawas, at the annual feast of Mylitta Anaitis, they sacrificed at Babylon the handsome slave who had just united with the priestess who incarnated the Assyrian goddess. This bloody religious ceremonial must have been a reproduction of an Amazonian custom.

The life of savagery and barbarism permits woman to develop her superiority from birth; each sex there has its special function; it is the division of labor in embryo. The man, whose muscular system is more developed, "fights, hunts, fishes and sits down," according to the Australian native, he regards all the rest as under the jurisdiction of woman, whose function puts brain activity into play at an earlier epoch. She has charge of the communal house, which often shelters a clan of more than one hundred individuals; she prepares clothing from skins and other raw materials; she charges herself with the cultivation of the garden, the rearing of domestic animals and the manufacture of household utensils; she preserves, economizes, cooks, distributes the provisions, vegetable and animal, which have been gathered during the course of the year; and like the Valkyries of the Scandinavians and the Keres of the pre-Homeric Greeks, she accompanies the warrior on the field battle, aids in the fray, raises him up if he is wounded and cares for him; her assistance is so appreciated that, according to Tacitus, the barbarians who under the leadership of Civilis revolted against Vespasian, were seized with pity for the Roman soldiers because their wives did not accompany them when they marched to combat. Plato likewise who, like the chosen ones initiated in the Eleusinian Mysteries, was more informed regarding ancient customs than is supposed, makes the women to be present in the battles of the warriors of his Republic.

These multiple and diverse functions, which obliged woman to reflect, to calculate, to think of the morrow and to look ahead at long range, must necessarily have developed her intellectual faculties; thus the craniologists say that only a slight difference exists between the cranial capacity of the two sexes in the negroes, the Australians, and the red skins, while they find that it goes on increasing among civilized people. Woman is for the careless and improvident savage, a providence; she is the prudent and prescient being who presides over his destinies from birth to death. Man, making his religions with the events and the intellectual acquisitions of his daily life, was thus obliged to begin by deifying woman. The pre-Homeric Greeks and Romans had placed their destinies under the control of goddesses, the Fates — Moirai, Parcae — whose name signifies in the Latin language "sparing," "economic," and in the Greek the part which falls to each one in the distribution of food or of booty.

If we relieve the rich and poetical Greek mythology of the symbolical, allegorical and mystical lucubrations with which the philosophers and the poets of the classical epoch and the Alexandrine period have overloaded and complicated it, and which the German mythologists, servilely copied by those of France and England, have carried on to their own more perfect confusion, it becomes an inestimable storehouse of prehistoric customs which preserves the memory of the manners which travelers and anthropologists now observe living again among the savages and barbarous nations of Africa and the New World. The mythological legend furnishes us with information of the relative value of feminine and masculine intelligence among the Greeks, before they had entered upon the patriarchal period.

Jupiter, the "father of the gods," as Homer, Hesiod and Aeschylos call him, after having driven the feminine divinities from Olympus, enthroned there the patriarchate, which for some generations had been established upon earth; the religious heaven always reflects terrestrial manners as the moon reflects the light of the sun. But Jupiter, who like every barbarian, knew how to use his fists (Iliad XV. 228), who boasted that he was the strongest of the gods, and who to dominate the others kept next his throne two servants, Force and Violence, always ready to obey his orders, was inadequately prepared by his intellectual qualities to replace woman in the government of the Olympian family; in order to supply the capacities which were lacking to him, Hesiod tells us that he married Metis, "the wisest among mortals and gods." The savage and the barbarian, that he may take into himself the courage of a fallen enemy, devours his throbbing heart; Jupiter carried off Metis to assimilate her cunning, her prudence and her wisdom, for her name in the Greek language has these diverse meanings; these qualities were considered as belonging to woman.

But the process of assimilation took some time, if we may judge from the rascally farce played upon him by Prometheus. The latter killed and butchered an enormous ox, in one pile he placed the flesh which he covered with the skin upon which he deposited the entrails; in another pile he put the bare bones which he adroitly concealed under heaps of fat. "You have divided the parts very badly," said the father of gods and men. "Most worthy Jupiter, greatest of living gods, take the part that your wisdom counsels you to choose," replied the astute Prometheus. The ruler of the heavens, listening only to his gluttony, laid both hands upon the heap of fat amid the laughter of the Olympians; his wrath was terrible when he saw the bare bones. (Theogony 435 *et seq.*) Such a farce would hardly have been played in the Olympian heaven had it not been that on the earth similar tests had been required to prove to the Father that his intellectual faculties did not justify him in taking the place of the Mother in the leadership of the family and the management of its property.

The higher position in the family and society, which man conquered by brute force, while it compelled him to a mental activity to which he was little accustomed, at the same time put at his disposal opportunities for reflection and development which constantly increased. Woman, "subdued," as the Greek expression has it, shut up in the narrow circle of the family, the leadership of which had been taken from her, and having little or no contact with the outside world, saw on the contrary a great reduction of the means of development which she had enjoyed, and to complete her subjection she was forbidden the intellectual culture which was given to man. If in spite of these fetters and these disadvantages, the disastrous effects of which cannot be exaggerated, the brain of woman continued to evolve, it was because woman's intelligence profited through the progress realized by the masculine brain; for one sex transmits to the other the qualities which it has acquired; thus pullets of certain varieties inherit the spurs which are highly developed among the cocks, while in other varieties they transmit to the males their exaggerated crests. "It is fortunate," says Darwin upon this point, "that the equal transmission of the characteristics of both sexes has been a general rule in the whole series of mammals, otherwise, it is probable that man would have become as superior to woman in intellectual power as the peacock is to the female in ornamental plumage." (Descent of Man — Sexual Selection, VIII and XIX.)

But defects as well as valuable qualities are transmitted from one sex to the other: if woman has profited by the brain-growth of man, he has in his turn been retarded in his development by the sluggishness in the development of woman's brain, produced by the reduction to the smallest minimum of intellectual activity to which he has condemned her. The breeders who seek the choicest results are as careful to have irreproachable females as males; amateur cockfighters attach as much importance to the selection of the pullets as to the cocks, they produce only from those which are armed with spurs and which have the fighting spirit. It may be said that humanity, since it emerged from communism of the clan to live under the system of private property, has been developed by the efforts of one sex alone and that its evolution has been retarded through the obstacles interposed by the other sex. Man by systematically depriving woman of the means of development, material and intellectual, has made of her a force retarding human progress.

In fact if we study and compare the different periods of savagery and barbarism, we cannot but observe the continuous and remarkable progress in human mind, because women and men, exercising freely their physical and mental faculties, contribute equally to the evolution of the species; this has been retarded ever since humanity entered into the period of civilization and private property, because then woman, constrained and confined in her development, cannot contribute to it in so effective a way. The senile stagnation in which China has vegetated for more than a thousand years can only be attributed to the degradation of woman, which has gone to the point of the cruel mutilation of her feet that she may be imprisoned the more closely in the woman's quarters. Europe also suffers from the degradation of woman, since in spite of the extraordinary material progress of these last two thousand years and the increasing and no less extraordinary accumulation of human knowledge, it cannot be maintained that the brain of the civilized modern exceeds in power and capacity that of the Greeks of the classic epoch, which extends from the seventh to the fourth century before the Christian era. It is certain that a Victor Hugo, a Zola, or any university graduate or doctor has stored in his brain an abundance of positive and diversified conceptions not possessed by Aeschylus, Anaxagoras, Protagoras and Aristotle, but that does not prove that his imagination and his intelligence, or that of his contemporaries is more rich, more varied and more vast than that of the generations of Ionia and Attica, who were the artificers of that incomparable budding and blossoming of science, philosophy, literature and art at which history marvels and who reveled in that subtle and paradoxical play of sophistical philosophy, the like of which has not again been seen. The sophists — Photagoras, Gorgias, Socrates, Plato, etc., stated, discussed and solved the problems of the spiritualistic philosophy and many others besides: yet the Hellenes of Asia Minor and of Greece had emerged from barbarism only a few centuries before. Many reasons may be cited to explain this arrest in human development, but the principal one is the subjection of woman.

IV.

Capitalist production, which takes charge of most of the labors to which woman devoted herself in the gentile house, has levied into its army of wage-workers in factory, shop, office and schoolroom, the wives and daughters of the working class and of the small bourgeoisie, in order to procure cheap labor. Its pressing need of intellectual capacities has set aside the venerable and venerated axiom of masculine ethics: "to read, write and count ought to be all of a woman's knowledge;" it has required that girls like boys be instructed in the rudiments of the sciences. The first step once taken, they could not be forbidden to enter the universities. They proved that the feminine brain, which the intellectuals had declared a "child's brain," was as capable as the masculine brain of receiving all scientific instruction. The abstract sciences (mathematics, geometry, mechanics, etc.), the first whose study had been accessible to woman, were also the first in which they could give the measure of their intellectual capacities; they are now attacking the experimental sciences (physiology, physics, chemistry, applied mechanics, etc), in America and Europe there arises a throng of women who are marching on a level with men in spite of the inferiority of the conditions of development in which they have lived since their first infancy.

As Capitalism has not snatched woman from the domestic hearth and launched her into social production to emancipate her, but to exploit her more ferociously than man, so it has been careful not to overthrow the economic, legal, political and moral barriers which had been raised to seclude her in the marital dwelling. Woman, exploited by capital, endures the miseries of the free laborer and bears in addition her chains of the past. Her economic misery is aggravated; instead of being supported by her father or husband, to whose rule she still submits, she is obliged to earn her living; and under the pretext that she has fewer necessities than man, her labor is paid less; and when her daily toil in the shop, the office or school is ended, her labor in the household begins. Motherhood, the sacred, the highest of social functions, becomes in capitalistic society a cause of horrible misery, economic and physiologic. The social and economic condition of woman is a danger for the reproduction of the species.

But this crushing and pitiful condition announces the end of her servitude, which begins with the establishment of private property and which can end only with its abolition. Civilized humanity, oppressed by the mechanical mode of production, turns its face toward a society, based on common property, in which woman, delivered from the economic, legal and moral chains which bind her, may develop freely her physical and intellectual faculties, as in the time of the communism of the savages.

The savages, to forbid primitive promiscuity and successfully restrain the circle of sexual relations, found no other means than to separate the sexes; there are reasons for believing that the women took the initiative in this separation, which the specialization of their functions consolidated and emphasized. This was manifested socially by religious ceremonials and secret languages peculiar to each set and even by struggles;* and after having taken the character of violent antagonism, it ended in the brutal subjection of woman, which still survives although it is progressively attenuated in proportion as the competition of the two sexes becomes more general and intense upon the economic field. But the modern antagonism will not end with the victory of one sex over the other, for it is one of the phenomena of the struggle of labor against capital, which will find its solution in the emancipation of the working class in which women as well as men are incorporated.

The technique of production which tends to suppress the specialization of trades and functions and to replace muscular effort by attention and intellectual skill and which, the more it is perfected, mingles and confounds man and woman the more in social labor, will prevent the return of the conditions which in savage and barbarous nations had maintained the separation of the sexes. Common property will put an end to the economic antagonism of specialization.

But if it is possible to catch a glimpse of the end of female servitude and of the antagonism

---

* A. W. Howit, who observed among the Australians a species of sexual totemism, says that it often happens that the women and men of one and the same clan fight, when the animal that serves as the totem for one sex is killed by the other sex.

of the sexes and to conceive for the human species an era of incomparable bodily and mental progress, brought about by women and men of a high development in muscle and brain, it is impossible to foresee the sexual relations of free and equal women and men who will not be united nor separated by sordid material interests and by the gross ethics engendered by such interests. But if we may judge by the present and the past, men, in whom the genetic passion is more violent and more continuous than in women — the same phenomenon is observed in the males and females of the whole animal series — will be obliged to exhibit their physical and intellectual qualities to win their sweethearts. Sexual selection, which, as Darwin has shown, fulfilled an important role in the development of the animal species and which, with rare exceptions, has ceased to play this part in the Indo-European races for about three thousand years, will again become one of the most active factors in the perfecting of the human race.

Motherhood and love will permit woman to regain the higher position which she occupied in primitive societies, the memory of which has been preserved by the legends and myths of the ancient religions.

THE SOCIALIST IDEAL

Our comrades in Germany were discussing some time since the question whether Socialism is a science. Socialism is not and cannot be a science for the simple reason that it is a political party and must disappear when its work is accomplished after the abolition of the classes which gave birth to it; but the end which it pursues is scientific.

Guizot, who had a vague idea of the theory of the class struggle—himself a product of the Revolution, which was a dramatic struggle between classes—said with good reason that a class cannot emancipate itself until it possesses the qualities requisite for taking the leadership of society; now one of these qualities is to have a more or less definite conception of the social order which it proposes to substitute for that which is oppressing it. This conception cannot but be a social ideal, or, to employ a scientific word, a social hypothesis; but an hypothesis, as well in the natural sciences as in social science, may be utopian or scientific.

Socialism, because it is a political party of the oppressed class, has therefore an ideal. It groups and organizes the efforts of the individuals who wish to build on the ruins of capitalist society, based upon individual property, an ideal or hypothetical society based upon common property in the means of production.

Only through the class struggle can modern socialism realize its social ideal, which possesses the qualities demanded of any hypothesis that claims a scientific character. The fact of choosing a scientific goal, and of trying to reach it only through the class struggle, distinguishes it from the Socialism of 1848, which was pursuing through the reconciliation of classes a social ideal which could not but be utopian considering the historic moment in which it was conceived. Socialism has thus evolved from Utopia into science. Engels has traced the main lines of this evolution in his memorable pamphlet, "Socialism, Utopian and Scientific." It is the same with all sciences, which begin with Utopia to arrive at positive knowledge; this course is imposed by the very nature of the human mind.

Man progresses in social life as in intellectual life, only by starting from the known and traveling toward the unknown, and that unknown must be represented by the imagination; that imaginary conception of the unknown, which cannot but be hypothetical, is one of the most powerful incentives to action, it is the very condition of every forward step. It is natural that men like Bernstein in Germany and Jaurès in France should seek to domesticate Socialism and to put it in tow of liberalism, accusing it of hypnotising its soldiers with an ideal of the year 3000, which makes them live in the expectation of a Messianic "catastrophe" and reject the immediate advantages of an understanding and cooperation with bourgeois parties, and which blinds them to their shocking errors regarding the concentration of wealth, the disappearance of small industry and the middle class, the increase of class antagonisms, the spreading and intensification of the misery of the working class, etc. These errors may have been plausible hypotheses before 1848, but since then events have shown their falsity. This unfortunate ideal prevents them from descending from the revolutionary heights to accept the responsibilities of power and of setting aside the cause of labor to devote themselves entirely tongue and pen, to the rehabilitation of a millionaire leader; it obliges them to oppose all exterior policies and acts, to vote not a cent nor a soldier for colonial expeditions, which carry labor, Christianity, syphilis and the alcoholism of civilization to the barbaric tribes. The neo-methodists of the ancient and outworn gospel of the brotherhood of classes advise the socialists to suppress their ideal, or, since it unfortunately captivates the masses of the people, to speak of it without caring for it, as Jaurès does, that they may consecrate themselves to practical necessities, to the vast plans of agricultural and industrial co-operation, to popular universities, etc.

The dilettantes of politics, these practical groundlings of opportunism, nevertheless hold themselves up for transcendent idealists and march with their eyes fixed upon the stars, because they substitute for ideas a brilliant orchestra of sonorous words and eternal principles.

These bourgeois idealists edge their way in everywhere; after the Revolution of 1789 they rebuked the scientists for their hypotheses and their theories; according to them science should have stopped with the study of facts in themselves without dreaming of uniting them into a general system. "What is the use of cutting stones without putting up a building," replied Geoffroy-Saint-Hilaire, the genial disciple of Lamarck, who lived to see the extinction of his theory on the continuity of species, which, only thirty years after his death, was to take on a new birth with Darwin. They are still reproaching the physiologists for wasting their time in elaborating hypotheses which last on an average only three years and which cannot explain what takes place in a muscle which contracts and in a brain which thinks. They grumble against the hypotheses of the physicists, who do not know the real nature of elasticity, of electrical conductivity, or even what happens when a particle of sugar is dissolved. They would like to prohibit scientists from any speculation because it is disastrous and may lead into error. But the latter protest and declare that imagination is one of the first and most indispensable faculties of the scientist, and that the hypotheses to which they give birth, even though they be erroneous and able to survive only three years, are nevertheless the necessary condition of all scientific progress.

If the communist ideal were an hypothesis undemonstrable and false it would still be a propelling force of social progress, but such is not the case.

The hypothesis in science, as in the social field, is the more undemonstrable and susceptible of error in proportion as the data contributing to its elaboration are less numerous and more uncertain. Greek science, which had to furnish a conception of the world when the data regarding the phenomena of nature were of the most rudimentary, was obliged to resort to hypotheses which for boldness and intuitive accuracy are marvels of history and of thought; after having admitted, according to the vulgar opinion, that the earth was flat, and that the temple of Delphi was situated at its center, they put forth the hypothesis of its spherical form, then undemonstrable.

Socialism, which dates from the first years of the nineteenth century, started, like Greek science, from hypotheses the more erroneous, and from ideal the more utopian, in that the social world which it proposed to transform was less known; and at that epoch could not be known for the excellent reason that it was in course of formation.

The machine operated by steam was beginning to edge into industry where the tool, managed by the artisan, was moved by human power, and in some rare circumstances by animals, wind or waterfalls. The Socialist thinkers, as Engels observes, were then obliged to draw from their own brain the social ideal which they could not extract from the tumultuous economic environment in full course of transformation. They grasped again, infusing new life into it, the communist ideal which has slumbered in the mind of man since he emerged from the communism of primitive society which the poetic Greek mythology calls the golden age and which has awakened to shine here and there with a glorious splendor at great epochs of social upheaval. They sought, then, to establish communism, not because the economic environment was ready for its introduction, but because men were miserable, because the laws of justice and equality were violated, because the precepts of the Christ could not be followed in their purity. The communistic ideal, not springing from economic reality, was then but an unconscious reminiscence of a prehistoric past, and came only from idealistic notions upon a justice, an equality and a gospel law no less idealistic; it is then idealistic in the second degree, and consequently utopian.

The Socialists of the first half of the nineteenth century, who rekindled the communist ideal, had the rare merit of giving it a consistency less idealistic. They spoke little of the Christian religion, of justice and of equality; Robert Owen laid the responsibilities of social evils upon the family, property and religion; Charles Fourier criticises the ideas of justice and morality introduced by the bourgeois Revolution of '89 with incomparable animation and irony. They did not weep over the misery of the poor, but left that to Victor Hugo and the charlatans of romanticism. They preached the social problem from its realistic side, the only side from which it can be solved. They used their talents to prove that a social organization of production would succeed in satisfying the desires of all without reducing the share of any, not even that of the privileged capitalist class. Meanwhile the recent application of steam and machinery demanded also a new organization of labor, and this was the constant concern of the industrial bourgeoisie. The socialists were thus pursuing the same end as the industrials; bourgeois and socialists might consequently come to an understanding. We therefore find in the socialist sects of that epoch industrials, engineers and financiers who in the second half of the century cast away their sympathy for the workers and occupied an important place in capitalist society.

The socialism of that epoch could not under these conditions be anything else than pacific; instead of entering on the struggle with the capitalists, the socialists thought only of converting them to their system of social reform from which they were to be the first to benefit.

They proclaimed the association of capital, intelligence and labor, the interests of which, according to them, were identical! they preached a mutual understanding between the employer and the employed, between the exploiter and the exploited; they know no class struggle; they condemned strikes and all political agitation, especially if it were revolutionary; they desired order in the street and harmony in the workshop. They demanded, finally, nothing more than was desired by the new industrial bourgeoisie.

They foresaw that industry, strengthened by the motive power of steam, machinery and the concentration of the instruments of labor, would have a colossal producing power, and they had the simplicity to believe that the capitalists would content themselves with taking only a reasonable part of the wealth thus created, and would leave to their co-operators, the manual and intellectual laborers, a portion sufficient to enable them to live in comfort. This socialism was marvellously agreeable to capital, since it promised an increase of wealth and advised an understanding between the laborer and the employer. It recruited the great majority of its adepts in the educational hotbeds of the bourgeoisie. It was utopian, therefore it was the socialism of the intellectuals.

But precisely because it was utopian, the laborers, in constant antagonism with their employers on questions of labor and hours, looked on it with suspicion. They could understand nothing of this socialism which condemned strikes and political action and which assumed to harmonize the interests of capital and labor, of the exploiter and exploited. They kept aloof from the socialists and gave all their sympathies to the bourgeois republicans, because they were revolutionary. They joined their secret societies and climbed with them upon the barricades to make riots and political revolutions.

Marx and Engels took socialism at the point to which the great utopians had brought it, but instead of torturing their brains to improvise the organization of labor and of production, they studied that which was already created by the very necessities of the new mechanical industry which had arrived at a degree of development sufficient to permit its power and its tendency to be apparent. Its productivity was so enormous, as Fourier and Saint Simon had foreseen, that it was capable of providing abundantly for the normal needs of all the members of society. This was the first time in history that such a productive power had been observed, and it was because capitalist production could satisfy all needs, and for that reason alone, that it is possible to reintroduce communism, that is to say the equal participation of all in social wealth, and the free and complete development of the physical, intellectual and moral faculties. Communism is no longer a utopia but a possibility.

Machinery replaces the individualistic production of the small industry, by the communistic production of the capitalistic factory, but property in the means of labor has remained individual, as in the time of the small industry. There is then a contradiction between the individualistic mode of possession and the communist mode of production and this contradiction translates itself into the antagonism between the laborer and the capitalist employer. The producers, who form the immense majority of the nation, no longer possess the instruments of labor, the possession of which is centralized in the idle hands of a decreasing minority. The social problem imposed by mechanical production will be solved, as the social problems imposed by preceding modes of production have been solved, by precipitating the evolution begun by economic force, by finishing the expropriation of the individual in the means of production, by giving to the communistic mode of production the communistic mode of possession which it demands.

The communism of contemporary socialists no longer proceeds, like that of former times, from the cerebral lucubrations of gifted thinkers; it proceeds from economic reality, it is the final goal of the economic forces which, without attracting the attention of the capitalists and their intellectuals, have fashioned the communistic mold of a new society, the coming of which we only have to hasten. Communism, then, is no longer a utopian hypothesis; it is a scientific ideal. It may be added that never has the economic structure of any society been better and more completely analyzed than capitalist society, and that never was a social ideal conceived with such numerous and positive data as the communist idea of modern socialism.

Although it is the economic forces which fashion men at the pleasure and spur them to action, and although these constitute the mysterious force determining the great currents of history which the Christians attribute to God, and the free-thinking bourgeois assign to Progress, to Civilization, to the Immortal Principles and other similar manitous, worthy of savage tribes, they are nevertheless the product of human activity. Man, who created them and brought them into the world, has thus far let himself be guided by them; yet now that he has understood their nature and grasped their tendency, he can act upon their evolution. The socialists who are accused of being stricken by Oriental fatalism and of relying upon the good pleasure of economic forces to bring to light the communist society instead of crossing their arms like the fakirs of official Economics, and of bending the knee before its fundamental dogma, *laissez faire, laissez passer,* propose on the contrary to subdue them, as the blind forces of nature have been subdued, and force them to do good to men instead of leaving them to work misery to the toilers of civilization. They do not wait for their ideal to fall from heaven as the Christians hope for the grace of God, and the capitalists for wealth; they prepare, on the contrary, to realize it, not by appealing to the intelligence of the capitalist class and to its sentiments of justice and humanity, but by fighting it, by expropriating it from its political power, which protects its economic despotism.

Socialism, because it possesses a social ideal, has in consequence a criticism of its own. Every class which struggles for its enfranchisement seeks to realize a social ideal, in complete opposition with that of the ruling class. The struggle is waged at first in the ideological world before the physical shock of the revolutionary battle. It thus begins the criticism of the ideas of the society which must be revolted against, for "the ideas of the ruling class are the ideas of society," or these ideas are the intellectual reflection of its material interests.

Thus, the wealth of the ruling class is produced by slave labor; religion, ethics, philosophy and literature agree in authorizing slavery. The ugly God of the Jews and Christianity strikes with his curse the progeny of Ham, that it may furnish slaves. Aristotle, the encyclopedic thinker of Greek philosophy, declares that slaves are predestined by nature and that no rights exist for them, for there can be no rights except between equals. Euripides in his tragedies preaches the doctrine of servile morality; St. Paul, St. Augustine and the Church teach slaves submission to their earthly masters that they may deserve the favor of their heavenly master; Christian civilization introduced slavery into America and maintains it there until economic phenomena prove that slave labor is a method of exploitation more costly and less profitable than free labor.

At the epoch when the Greco-Roman civilization was dissolving, when the labor of artisans and free workers began to be substituted for slave labor, pagan religion, philosophy and literature decided to accord them certain rights. The same Euripides who advised the slave to lose his personality in that of the master does not wish him to be despised. "There is nothing shameful in slavery but the name," says the pedagogue in Ion, "the slave, moreover, is not inferior to the free man when he has a noble heart." The mysteries of Eleusis and of Orphism, like Christianity, which continues their work, admit slaves among their initiated and promise them liberty, equality and happiness after death.

The dominating class of the Middle Ages being military, the Christian religion and social ethics condemned lending money at interest, and covered the lender with infamy; to take interest for money loaned was then something so ignominious that the Jewish race, obliged to specialize itself in the trade of money, still bears the shame of it. But to-day, now that the Christians have become Jews, and the ruling class lives on the interest of its capital, the trade of the lender at interest is the most honorable, the most desirable, the most exclusive.

The oppressed class, although the ideology of the oppressing class is imposed upon it, nevertheless elaborates religious, ethical and political ideas corresponding to its condition of life; vague and secret at first, they gain in precision and force in proportion as the oppressed class takes definite form and acquires the consciousness of its social utility and of its strength; and the hour of its emancipation is near when its conception of nature and of society opposes itself openly and boldly to that of the ruling class.

The economic conditions in which the bourgeois moves and evolves make of it a class essentially religious. Christianity is its work and will last as long as this class shall rule society. Seven or eight centuries before Christ, when the bourgeoisie had its birth in the commercial and industrial cities of the Mediterranean sea, we may observe the elaboration of a new religion; the gods of paganism created by warrior tribes could not be suited to a class consecrated to the production and sale of merchandise. Mysterious cults (the mysteries of the Cabiri, of Demeter, of Dionysus, etc.) revive the religious traditions of the prehistoric matriarchical period; the idea of a soul and its existence after death revive; the idea of posthumous punishments and rewards to compensate for acts of social injustice are introduced, etc. These religious elements, combined with the intellectual data of

Greek philosophy, contribute to form Christianity, the religion, *par excellence,* of societies which have for their foundation property belonging to the individual and the class which enrich themselves by the exploitation of wage labor. For fifteen centuries all the movements of the bourgeoisie, either for organization, or for selfemancipation, or for the acquisition of power have been accompanied and complicated by religious crises; but always Christianity more or less modified remains the religion of society. The revolutionists of 1789, who in the ardor of the struggle promised themselves to de-Christianize France, were eager when the bourgeoisie were victorious to raise again the altars they had overthrown and to reintroduce the cult that they had proscribed.

The economic environment which produces the proletariat relieves it on the contrary from every idea of sentiment. There is not seen either in Europe nor in America among the laboring masses of the great industries any anxiety to elaborate a religion to replace Christianity, nor any desire to reform it. The economic and political organizatons of the working class are completely uninterested as to any doctrinal discussion of religious and spiritual dogmas, although they combat the priests of all cults because they are the lackeys of the capitalist class.

The victory of the proletariat will deliver humanity from the nightmare of religion. The belief in superior beings to explain the natural world and the social inequality, and to prolong the dominion of the ruling class, and the belief in the posthumous existence of the soul to recompense the inequality of fate will have no more justification once man, who has already grasped the general causes of the phenomena of nature, shall live in a communist society from whence shall have disappeared the inequality and the injustice of capitalistic society.

The militant socialists, following the example of the encyclopedists of the eighteenth century, have to make a merciless criticism of the economic, political, historical, philosophical, moral and religious ideas of the capitalist class in order to prepare in all spheres of thought the triumph of the new ideology which the proletariat introduces into the world.

THE RIGHTS OF THE HORSE AND THE RIGHTS OF MAN

Capitalist Civilization has endowed the wage-worker with the metaphysical Rights of Man, but this is only to rivet him more closely and more firmly to his economic duty.

"I make you free," so speak the Rights of Man to the laborer, "free to earn a wretched living and turn your employer into a millionaire; free to sell him your liberty for a mouthful of bread. He will imprison you ten hours or twelve hours in his workshops; he will not let you go till you are wearied to the marrow of your bones, till you have just enough strength left to gulp down your soup and sink into a heavy sleep. You have but one of your rights that you may not sell, and that is the right to pay taxes.

Progress and Civilization may be hard on wage-working humanity, but they have all a mother's tenderness for the animals which stupid bipeds call "lower."

Civilization has especially favored the equine race: it would be too great a task to go through the long list of its benefactions; I will name but a few, of general notoriety, that I may awaken and inflame the passionate desires of the workers, now torpid in their misery.

Horses are divided into distinct classes. The equine aristocracy enjoys so many and so oppressive privileges, that if the human-faced brutes which serve them as jockeys, trainers, stable valets and grooms were not morally degraded to the point of not feeling their shame, they would have rebelled against their lords and masters, whom they rub down, groom, brush and comb, also making their beds, cleaning up their excrements and receiving bites and kicks by way of thanks.

Aristocratic horses, like capitalists, do not work; and when they exercise themselves in the fields they look disdainfully, with a coupon-clipper's contempt, upon the human animals which plow and seed the lands, mow and rake the meadows, to provide them with oats, clover, timothy and other succulent plants.

These four-footed favorites of Civilization command such social influence that they impose their wills upon the capitalists, their brothers in privilege; they force the loftiest of them to come with their beautiful ladies and take tea in the stables, inhaling the acrid perfumes of their solid and liquid evacuations. And when these lords consent to parade in public, they require from ten to twenty thousand men and women to stack themselves up on uncomfortable seats, under the broiling sun, to admire their exquisitely chiseled forms and their feats of running and leaping. They respect none of the social dignities before which the votaries of the Rights of Man bow in reverence. At Chantilly not long ago one of the favorites for the grand prize launched a kick at the king of Belgium, because it did not like the looks of his head. His royal majesty, who adores horses, murmured an apology and withdrew.

It is fortunate that these horses, who can count more authentic ancestors than the houses of Orleans and Hohenzollern, have not been corrupted by their high social station: had they taken it into their heads to rival the capitalists in aesthetic pretentions, profligate luxury and depraved tastes, such as wearing lace and diamonds, and drinking champagne and Chateau-Margaux, a blacker misery and more overwhelming drudgery would be impending over the class of wage-workers.

Thrice happy is it for proletarian humanity

that these equine aristocrats have not taken the fancy of feeding upon human flesh, like the old Bengal tigers which rove around the villages of India to carry off women and children; if unhappily the horses had been man-eaters, the capitalists, who can refuse them nothing, would have built slaughter-houses for wage-workers, where they could carve out and dress boy sirloins, woman hams and girl roasts to satisfy their anthropophagic tastes.

The proletarian horses, not so well endowed, have to work for their peck of oats, but the capitalist class, through deference for the aristocrats of the equine race, concedes to the working horses rights that are far more solid and real than those inscribed in the "Rights of Man."

The first of rights, the right to existence, which no civilized society will recognize for laborers, is possessed by horses.

The colt, even before his birth, while still in the fetus state, begins to enjoy the right to existence; his mother, when her pregnancy has scarcely begun, is discharged from all work and sent into the country to fashion the new being in peace and comfort; she remains near him to suckle him and teach him to choose the delicious grasses of the meadow, in which he gambols until he is grown.

The moralists and politicians of the "Rights of Man" think it would be monstrous to grant such rights to the laborers; I raised a tempest in the Chamber of Deputies when I asked that women, two months before and two months after confinement, should have the right and the means to absent themselves from the factory. My proposition upset the ethics of civilization and shook the capitalist order. What an abominable abomination—to demand for babies the rights of colts.

As for the young proletarians, they can scarcely trot on their little toes before they are condemned to hard labor in the prisons of capitalism, while the colts develop freely under kindly Nature; care is taken that they be completely formed before they are set to work, and their tasks are proportioned to their strength with a tender care.

This care on the part of the capitalists follows them all through their lives. We may still recall the noble indignation of the bourgeois press when it learned that the omnibus company was using peat and tannery waste in its stalls as a substitute for straw: to think of the unhappy horses having such poor litters! The more delicate souls of the bourgeoisie have in every capitalist country organized societies for the protection of animals, in order to prove that they can not be excited by the fate of the small victims of industry. Schopenhauer, the bourgeois philosopher, in whom was incarnated so perfectly the gross egoism of the philistine, could not hear the cracking of a whip without his heart being torn by it.

This same omnibus company, which works its laborers from fourteen to sixteen hours a day, requires from its dear horses only five to seven hours. It has bought green meadows in which they may recuperate from fatigue or indisposition. Its policy is to expend more for the entertainment of a quadruped than for paying the wages of a biped. It has never occurred to any legislator nor to any fanatical advocate of the "Rights of Man" to reduce the horse's daily pittance in order to assure him a retreat that would be of service to him only after his death.

The Rights of Horses have not been posted up; they are "unwritten rights," as Socrates called the laws implanted by Nature in the consciousness of all men.

The horse has shown his wisdom in contenting himself with these rights, with no thought of demanding those of the citizen; he has judged that he would have been as stupid as man if he had sacrificed his mess of lentils for the metaphysical banquet of Rights to Revolt, to Equality, to Liberty, and other trivialities which to the proletariat are about as useful as a cautery on a wooden leg.

Civilization, though partial to the equine race, has not shown herself indifferent to the fate of the other animals. Sheep, like canons, pass their days in pleasant and plentiful idleness; they are fed in the stable on barley, lucerne, rutabagas and other roots, raised by wage-workers; shepherds conduct them to feed in fat pastures, and when the sun parches the plain, they are carried to where they can browse on the tender grass of the mountains.

The Church, which has burned her heretics, and regrets that she can not again bring up her faithful sons in the love of "mutton," represents Jesus, under the form of a kind shepherd, bearing upon his shoulders a weary lamb.

True, the love for the ram and the ewe is in the last analysis only the love for the leg of mutton and the cutlet, just as the Liberty of the Rights of Man is nothing but the slavery of the wage-worker, since our jesuitical Civilization always disguises capitalist exploitation in eternal principles and bourgeois egoism in noble sentiments; yet at least the bourgeois tends and fattens the sheep up to the day of the sacrifice, while he seizes the laborer still warm from the workshop and lean from toil to send him to the shambels of Tonquin or Madagascar.

Laborers of all crafts, you who toil so hard to create your poverty in producing the wealth of the capitalists, arise, arise! Since the buffoons of parliament unfurl the Rights of Man, do you boldly demand for yourselves, your wives and your children the Rights of the Horse.

THE END.

Printed in the United States
101456LV00001B/139/A